VAMPIRES AMONG US

Here are the stories of . . . Kevin, who was part of a strange and erotic vampire threesome . . . Judith, a freelance writer, whose youthful fascination with vampires turned to reality one night . . . Rose, a mild-mannered schoolteacher and blood fetishist . . . Damien, who roams London in full "vampire drag"—head-to-foot black clothes accented with silver crosses, crucifixes, chains and rings—and says that in a past life, she was guillotined for being a witch . . . and many more . . .

ROSEMARY ELLEN GUILEY is a journalist and author of several works on paranormal phenomena, including *Tales of Reincarnation*, published by Pocket Books. She is a member of the American Society of Psychical Research and the Society for Psychical Research, London.

Books by Rosemary Ellen Guiley

Angels of Mercy
Tales of Reincarnation
Vampires Among Us

Published by POCKET BOOKS

VAMPIRES
AMONG US

ROSEMARY
ELLEN
GUILEY

POCKET BOOKS

New York   London   Toronto   Sydney   Tokyo   Singapore

An *Original* Publication of POCKET BOOKS

POCKET BOOKS, a division of Simon & Schuster Inc.
1230 Avenue of the Americas, New York, NY 10020

ISBN: 0-671-72361-8

First Pocket Books printing August 1991

10 9 8 7 6 5 4

POCKET and colophon are registered trademarks of
Simon & Schuster Inc.

Cover photo by Roger Tully

Printed in the U.S.A.

For Jeanne K. Youngson

obstupui steteruntque comae

Acknowledgments

I would like to express my gratitude to those who helped bring this book into being. First and foremost, thanks to Scott Siegel, who conceived the idea for the book, and to Claire Zion, associate executive editor at Pocket Books, who commissioned it.

In my research, I was aided by many individuals who shared their expertise, their own researches, and contributed their experiences. I am especially grateful to Jeannie Youngson, founder and president of the Count Dracula Fan Club, to whom this book is dedicated. Jeannie gave me frequent access to the wealth of material in the club archives and was instrumental in helping me contact others. I would also like to thank the following individuals who were generous with their time and expertise: Eric S. Held, cofounder of the Vampire Information Exchange; Martin V. Riccardo, founder and director of Vampires Studies; John L. Vellutini, founder and editor of the *Journal of Vampirology;* Allen J. Gittens, founder and president of the original Vampyre Society; Bernard Davies, cofounder and honorable chairman of The Dracula Society; and Vincent Hillyer, author and arcanalogist. A special salute goes to Sean Manchester, founder and president of the International Society of Irreproducible Vampire and Lycanthropy

Research, and founder of the Grail Church, for a memorable afternoon at Highgate Cemetery in London. In addition, Margaret L. Carter provided perspectives on the fictional image of the vampire. Stephen Kaplan, founder and director of the Vampire Research Center, gave me information on the collection of data concerning self-professed vampires.

I also would like to express my gratitude to all those who gave me their vampire experiences. For reasons of privacy, names and other identifying details have been changed for many of them. Thanks again to all of you.

I also thank Karen Sue Powell-Chapman, for granting permission to quote from her copyrighted dream journals in Chapter Nine. Some of the excerpts appeared previously in print in *Coven Journal*. Thanks also to Sean Manchester for granting permission to quote from his book *The Highgate Vampire* in Chapter Five.

Finally, I would like to thank Margaret Guiley for assisting me with library research, and Barbara Gorrell and Joanne P. Austin for helping me with the transcriptions of interview tapes.

Regrettably, a promising organization for fans of vampire film and fiction passed from the scene during the course of my research. The Children of the Night, founded by Thomas P. and Michele Strauch of Evergreen Park, Illinois, launched an exciting and polished publication, *Coven Journal*. Alas, membership income could not cover production costs—a problem faced by many fan organizations—and The Children of the Night came to an end in the summer of 1990.

Contents

Introduction

Welcome to Vampire Reality, a world in which vampires—*real* vampires—can exist. It is a state of being, a state of mind, an alternate reality that interpenetrates the "ordinary" reality of everyday life. As you spend your time in routine pursuits of working, eating, sleeping, and relaxing, someone next to you, in the next room, the next apartment, the next house, the next town, is living a very different life, perhaps a secret life, in Vampire Reality.

Who are those in Vampire Reality? They are living vampires, as real and as flesh-and-blood as you. They are the Undead, vampires who rise from the grave. They are spirit vampires. They are fantasy vampires and dream vampires. They are also vampire witnesses and vampire victims, vampire hunters and vampire researchers.

Vampire Reality is like a kaleidoscope—multi-faceted, full of constantly shifting prisms of colors and shapes. Like a kaleidoscope, it offers particular patterns to one person and one person only: the beholder. The same might be said about ordinary reality, for although we live according to a collectively defined universe, each of us has deep within the heart a set of truths, beliefs, and perspectives that shape a personal universe. Each of us lives according to a truth as we see it.

Those who enter Vampire Reality see it from their own unique perspectives, from their own truths. Vampire Reality for one person is different from Vampire Reality for another. There is no right or wrong, just difference.

Some people live full-time in Vampire Reality. Others make excursions there, when they dream, when they fantasize, and when they have unexpected encounters with the unknown.

It is possible to visit Vampire Reality. We're going to go there and see it from the varied perspectives of those who live there and those who've been there and back—vampires, vampire victims, hunters, researchers, and dreamers among them.

VAMPIRES
AMONG US

Chapter One

They Call Themselves Vampires

My own search for vampires took me around the United States and across the Atlantic to England. Before I could begin, I had to establish what exactly I was looking for.

Webster's Ninth New Collegiate Dictionary defines *vampire* as "the reanimated body of a dead person believed to come from the grave at night and suck the blood of persons asleep." However, this is by no means the last word.

If you ask people to define a vampire, you get different answers. Most will follow Webster's lead, tempering it with a generous dose of influence from popular fiction and film: a resurrected corpse who is immortal, physically and sexually attractive, sophisticated, nocturnal in habit, and the possessor of great and supernatural powers—and who is evil, of course, because of the need to prey upon humans for blood. Or you will hear that a vampire is a living human being who drinks blood, or requires blood in order to

1

live, but is not necessarily supernatural or immortal. The fact is, however, that both of these popular definitions have little in common with their source, the "real" vampire of folklore.

But pinning down the "real" vampire is not easy, either, for the folkloric vampire varies greatly in description, nature, and behavior and goes by many different names, each of which carries a unique connotation. The vampires of Slavic folklore—who will be examined in greater detail in Chapter Three—were variously described as reanimated corpses, spirits of the dead, demons, living human beings with a need for blood, and supernatural humans, werewolf-like creatures, or witches who possessed the power to shape-shift into animals.

Thus, there is no one vampire that sets the standard by which all other alleged vampires can be measured and qualified. Consequently, the vampire is capable of constantly reinventing itself and thrives in many guises in the collective human psyche.

As a result, I decided to look inside Vampire Reality and see how vampires manifest, and how their manifestation affects human beings.

I did not expect to find reanimated corpses, or replicas of Bram Stoker's Count Dracula or Anne Rice's Lestat, Louis, and Armand. Such vampires truly are fantasy—they are a projection of wishful thinking about what constitutes a "real" vampire.

I envisioned my ideal vampire to be in some way supernatural or to show some involvement in an alternate reality. That is, there would be circumstances or phenomena associated with the vampire that defied, or appeared to defy, natural explanation.

This standard ruled out blood fetishists, individuals who have a craving or liking for the consumption of blood, human or animal. They may simply like the taste of blood, or enjoy it as part of sex, or use it in magical rites, or drink it because they believe that it imparts health, longevity, or magical powers. Most such people are blood-drinkers, pure and simple, and have no connection to the supernatural or to folkloric vampirism. At best, they are "vampirelike," because, like the vampire, they consume blood.

Also ruled out were killers who called themselves vampires. There are numerous cases of individuals who apparently have murdered others in acts of violence that included drinking the blood of their victims. These people aren't really "vampires" either, since for them blood-drinking is secondary to the act of killing.

Finally, I ruled out sufferers of pernicious anemia and porphyria, blood disorders that cause cravings for blood. Illnesses simply don't count.

I did find men and women who professed to be vampires; that is, they believed they were no longer entirely human. Most said they were turned into vampires by other individuals who were vampires, in rituals that usually involved the exchange of blood. None of them claimed to be hundreds of years old, though most believed that their aging process had slowed due to their unique state of being. None claimed to be able to shape-shift or fly, though many felt their physical abilities and senses were enhanced by vampirism. Some professed to have the vampire's phobias as described in folklore, such as the fear of garlic and an inability to cross running water, yet others did not. In fact, a great deal of inconsistency existed in the claims made about what vampires can and cannot do.

None of the self-professed vampires offered proof or even tangible evidence that they had altered their human condition by becoming vampires. It must be pointed out that none of them had ever submitted to a medical or scientific examination; none probably would even consider doing so. Those who become vampires believe in the reality of their own transformations, and feel no need to prove it to anyone else.

Despite the lack of physical evidence, I was intrigued by the extent to which a life becomes reordered and reorganized after transformation. Those who believe themselves to be vampires begin living according to their perceptions, both conscious and subconscious, of how vampires should live. They become more nocturnal, more secretive, more sensitive to sunlight; they search out like-minded individuals with whom they can share blood and the vampire life. Generally, they feel these changes are the externally caused results of the transformation and are out of their control. It is possible, and perhaps even likely, that the changes occur because of a powerful, internal expectation concerning how vampires "should" be. Regardless of what may cause the changes, the changes themselves reinforce the belief in the transformation from human to vampire. Such individuals truly begin to live in Vampire Reality.

I have included several accounts of such vampire transformations, including one that allegedly involved the participation of vampires who exist in the spirit realm. The stories give a range of viewpoints and experiences. They show the similarities and differences in how vampires allegedly come into being, how they are constituted, and how they behave. Some cases may seem to strain credibility, but are of interest in showing a variety of lifestyles of self-professed vampires.

I was also intrigued by people who felt they had experienced an encounter with a vampire. These vampires took various forms, from living humans to invisible spirits or entities. Some were "psychic vampires," individuals or entities who seemed to have the power to invisibly attack human beings and suck away their vital energy.

Many of the encounters described to me were curious and seemed to have supernatural elements, such as the dramatic case of the vampires who manifested through a Ouija board, described in Chapter Seven, or the vampire attacks described in Chapter Eight. But as any student of the paranormal knows, it is often easy to come up with a natural explanation for something that appears to defy explanation. Ultimately, each of us has to weigh and assess the facts and come to our own conclusions.

My own belief is that it is possible to have an encounter with the unknown when the "psychic atmosphere" is right. That is, the event occurs at a moment when an individual is in a certain place and possessing a certain frame of mind. Some people seem to be more open to the unseen than others, or may simply be more receptive if psychological conditions are right. For example, two people can enter an allegedly haunted house, and one person will sense the presence of ghosts and the other will feel nothing.

Furthermore, I think it is likely that at least some encounters with the unknown will take a form that fits cultural beliefs. For example, in parts of the world where there are long traditions of fairy folk and these beliefs are still psychically active, it is not uncommon to hear of sightings of, or meetings with, the little people. In medieval times, there were reports of encounters with the Devil. We don't hear much about confronting the Devil as a physical being today—people instead are meeting extraterrestrials and vampires. Both are as real today as the Devil was centuries ago.

Some argue that all of these figures are nothing more than projections from the unconscious that take on the appearance of external reality. The great psychiatrist Carl G. Jung developed the concept of the collective unconscious, which is a layer of the human psyche. Jung said that below our waking state is the personal unconscious, our own unique memories and repressed material. Below that is the collective unconscious, shared by all humanity since the beginning of our time. The collective unconscious is a reservoir of primal memories and patterns of behavior, or archetypes. Archetypes—something Jung never precisely defined—come to our attention in the waking state in various forms. They are images that surface in our dreams, religions, myths, art, literature, and folklore. At times they can become projected to appear to exist on their own. The Devil is a representation of an archetype, embodying evil. The Great Mother is a representation of an archetype, embodying the ongoing cycle of birth, death, and rebirth. The vampire, too, can reside in the collective unconscious. In the following chapters we shall see what the vampire appears to embody.

Not everyone agrees that encounters with the unknown are merely projections from the personal and collective unconsciousnesses. The opposing argument is made that all encounters must be taken at face value, and that the entities exist independently in an external and alternate reality.

The truth probably lies somewhere in between.

It is evident that the vampire is indeed a powerful image in the collective unconscious of our modern society, drawing continual reinforcement from film, fiction, advertising, and pop culture. Some vampire encounters may be shaped by a person's great personal interest in the vampire. But vampire encounters also can occur to those who consciously pay scant attention to the vampire, yet are influenced subconsciously by the culture at large.

Literary inventions have had a powerful influence on our collective impression of the vampire. In fiction and film, the vampire has acquired characteristics, powers, and flaws that never existed in folklore. Since most people today derive all or part of their impressions about vampires from film and fiction, I expected to find modern vampires with literary characteristics.

Eastern European folklore accounts provide various descriptions of vampires (see Chapter Three). For the most part, vampires are said to be spirits of the dead, reanimated corpses, or infernal entities that attack, drain, and kill the living. They are fetid, foul things. Those that rise from the grave in one form or another feed on the living in order to maintain an incorrupt body in the coffin. Garlic, iron, silver, and various kinds of wood are among universal folklore remedies against evil in general, and are not limited to vampires.

There is very little in Eastern European folklore

that associates vampires with bats. We may thank Bram Stoker, author of *Dracula* (1897), for popularizing the notion that vampires turn into bats. Other attributes and characteristics of vampires that are literary inventions include living among humans in a physical body, the need to sleep in native earth, sensitivity to or inability to tolerate sunlight, superior senses and physical strength, immortality in a physical form, immunity to disease and illness, and fast healing of wounds. Of course, a keen intellect, sophisticated tastes, elegant clothing, and nights out at the opera are literary inventions, too.

All these attributes and more are part of the collectively held image of the vampire in modern culture. Thus, when a vampire manifests—whether it is someone becoming a vampire or someone encountering a vampire—the experience is likely to be shaped by the collective image. True to my expectations, the true modern vampire stories I found invariably contained elements of both folklore and fiction.

All of the individuals presented in this book have had experiences that to them are real. By attempting to look for possible influences and explanations, I do not mean to imply that any of these experiences were not real. Ultimately, we create our own reality from our own experiences and beliefs—which is why it is even possible for Vampire Reality to exist.

Individuals who call themselves vampires are not common, but I found they could be located by looking in the right places and making the right inquiries. Some of my subjects were open about their vampirism, to the extent that they have become media personalities. Most, however, remained secretive, guarding their privacy ferociously. Except for keeping strange hours and perhaps, but not always, showing a preference for dressing in black, these living vampires have managed to skirt the edges of ordinary reality and carry on in the workaday world. Others may consider them unusual or eccentric or reclusive, but not necessarily a supernatural threat to humanity. In fact, most living vampires won't go looking for trouble. Some do sally forth on nocturnal prowls for blood, but by and large these vampires said they prefer to carry on their vampiric activities quietly with others of like mind. They may occasionally attempt to seduce an ordinary mortal into their lifestyle, or yield to the entreaties of a mortal who wishes to be turned into a vampire. They see themselves as a special breed. But you can judge for yourself from their stories.

The vampires I encountered varied in their willingness to talk about themselves. Some revealed a little, others a great deal. Some were reluctant to be taped in an interview, but were terrific letter-writers and poured their souls onto paper. With few exceptions, their views on Vampire Reality were both intriguing and haunting. No two viewpoints were quite the same.

Confessions of a Young Vampire

Kevin [a pseudonym] is a young vampire in his thirties who lives on the East Coast of the United States. Here is his story in his own words:

My story begins about eight years ago, when I was working at the ——— school. I became friends with a man who happened to be very interested in the occult and,

9

among other things, vampirism. Mike [a pseudonym] was very knowledgeable and I loved his company. What made our relationship special was the fact that he convinced me that he was a vampire. He had jet black hair and his skin was very pale. He wore makeup on his face to give it some color.

I had met him through this young lady, Lisa [a pseudonym]. At the time she was having a relationship with Mike. My relationship with Lisa was strictly platonic, but Mike and I became sort of involved. Lisa wasn't jealous, really. She seemed rather amused by the whole thing.

I remember Lisa telling me that when she had sex with Mike, there was no intercourse, no penetration involved. It was mostly mutual masturbation and oral sex.

He did the same thing with me. (It was funny, really—when he was done with her, he'd come down the steps and then it was my turn.) I never made him come throughout our entire relationship. He insisted on doing everything, always. That disturbed me about him.

Lisa told me that she saw lights flashing when he was having sex with her, but I didn't experience that. I would, however, get extremely tired when he caressed me. He had that ability.

I never knew how he managed it, but he was able to take energy from me. I could feel it going out of me when we were playing around in a physical way—like when he would hold me down and tickle me or something (he was very strong for his size) and I'd feel myself getting weak and tired quickly, while he appeared to be getting a rush of adrenaline.

I remember one morning at his place. I had a lot of things to do, but I couldn't seem to wake up. He stayed close to me as we talked for a while, and I soon began to feel very awake and energetic, and I noticed that he had become so tired that he had to go back to bed.

No one would believe me when I talked about feelings I had when I was with him, so after a while I kept it to myself.

Mike had a friend, he said, who he went out with at night. They would go together to "feed," to drink human blood. I didn't know who his friend was, and I was a little jealous. He knew I wanted to try it, but he never let me go with him.

We were sitting in the park once, and I had a feeling that

he wanted to feed. His eyes changed color. They became a very bright green. I never forgot it because I had had some doubts about his being a vampire until this happened. I said to him, "Mike . . . your eyes!" and he got this wild expression on his face then and started laughing.

Once I let him bite me.

He had introduced me to this girl at the school. We were very interested in each other and Mike was friends with both of us. The night he introduced me to her, the three of us went out and bought some vodka and soda and we all took off from work or school for the night. We [all three of us] were having sex in her room when he bit me. He sucked my blood for a long time and I really loved the feeling this gave me. It was so warm and affectionate.

I think that experience has something to do with what I've been going through lately.

At the moment I'm living in a subbasement apartment in a suburb of ———. I keep the black blinds in my room closed constantly, and it really bothers me when guests open them and let in the daylight. I like to keep my room cool and dark nowadays. I wasn't always like that. It seems to have happened naturally, like some other things seem to have happened naturally.

Recently I had a problem walking over the ——— Bridge. I've crossed it hundreds of times without any problem whatsoever, but the last time I got to the middle and I became very afraid. I was really afraid to look at the water. I just looked down at the pavement until I got to the other side. I felt so vulnerable out in the middle of the bridge that I never want to cross it on foot again.

My walk is different now. I'm racing around all the time. My stride is wider than it used to be—I didn't even realize it until a few months ago. The walk I have now is just like Mike's walk. I could never keep up with him before. Now it wouldn't be a problem.

The strangest thing is that I really crave human blood. I want it so bad that I can feel the gums preparing for the bite. I suck them until they start to bleed. When the craving is really bad I get a "pressure" feeling on my eyes, like they're being held open by something. I also get the feeling that

11

trees and grass are vibrating with life and that they're "observing" me as I race past them.

Sometimes I wonder if I am losing my mind. No one would believe my feelings. Sometimes I think there things that I'm not dealing with and I'm retreating into some bizarre fantasy world where these problems transform themselves into something I *can* deal with. Loneliness becomes less troublesome, and blood becomes my link to others and the food that cures all.

Still, why this? Because I idolized Mike all those years? Can my personality be so weak that I have to resort to imitating others to get attention, even to the point where I don't know I'm doing it? No—I'm not really imitating Mike. I'm sure he was a vampire, but we had different experiences. The things that are happening to me seem to be happening in stages— as if they were supposed to come with age. But they don't with anyone else I know.

My goal now is to find other vampires. I know it will take a while, but that's okay with me.

I'm extremely careful when I "screen" people—because of the AIDS scare—and I'm sure other people like me are every bit as cautious.

What bothers me most of all is that I can't explain any of these things to my best friend. I've tried to talk to him about some things, but he doesn't understand it at all, and I know he never will.

Becoming a Vampire: A Dream Come True

As Kevin points out, the vampire's life is often a lonely one. Mortal friends either cannot be confided in, or, if they are, they do not understand Vampire Reality. Life is much happier if the vampire has a small circle of vampire confidants. Judith [a pseudonym], a writer from Lancashire, England, has enjoyed such company. She told me:

I have long been interested in vampires, since my teenage years. After seeing a vampire film, I loved the vampire. But it wasn't until last year that my interest returned.

I began to write a book about vampires, and it was during my research for the book that I met and became friends with two real vampires. I met them when I stayed with a couple of friends in North Wales. I happened to say to one of them that I was writing a book about vampires. To my delight, he told me he knew two real vampires and that they were to visit the next weekend. Soon it was arranged that I should come along the following weekend. And it was then that I met Martin and Cathy [not their real names]. It was an honor, as they don't meet just anyone. I was a little nervous to begin with, but when Martin sat next to me and began to talk to me, I started to feel more relaxed and so I asked him about himself.

After a while he looked me right in the eyes and said, "May I take some, just a little, for my energies are low at the moment?" I said yes; then he put his arm around me and leaned over. It was such a wonderful feeling, but all too soon it was over.

This more than anything convinced me that he really was a vampire.

At our first meeting we got on so well that they asked me to spend the weekend with them. It was on this visit that I just had to ask them if they would make me a vampire, too, and to my joy they did. I shall always love Martin and Cathy for that. They agreed, but only after telling me of the disadvantages and making sure I understood that it would be for life. All was made ready.

I was ever so pleased, for this was what I had dreamed of for so long and it was going to happen that night.

The transition was loving, sexy, and gentle. Martin was so loving as he laid me down on the bed. We made love, and then he said softly in my ear, "Now I will bite, and you shall then sleep, sleep as one of the dead, but you shall dream." Then he lowered his head. I held him close until unable to keep my eyes open any longer, succumbed, and slept. The next morning I awoke to find that I had been covered up, and

Cathy was asking if I was all right. Later the dear lady allowed me to take my nourishment from her.

Martin told me that he was bitten by a lovely lady vampire once, and enjoyed it so much that he asked her to do it again. It was he who made dear Cathy into one also. This is all he has told me.

First let me say that I do not drink blood. A little is tasted during the transition, but it is only a taste, nothing more. I take positive energies—sexual energies are the best kind, for they are positive energies and positive energies are very beneficial to us. They restore my vitality. I don't need to have sex to feed, I can and do take it by touch. I can now heal, by taking the negative energies. I have recently healed a friend of mine who had been very ill with a nervous disorder.

We do live longer, but as to how long, that is in the lap of the gods.

The disadvantages, I would say, would be the weakness when I need to take nourishment and cannot find the right kind of person. For you see, it must be someone younger than I for me to feel any benefit from it. I can take it from an older person, but I would need to take quite a bit of it to do me any good.

The other disadvantage is that now I have to wear sunglasses even when the sun isn't too bright.

Apart from my sensitivity to sunlight, the only other way my body has changed is that my fingernails have grown longer and also my hair. I also have lost a little weight.

But after saying all that, I am not sorry that I have become a vampire. It was what I always wanted, and I shall always love Martin and Cathy for their most wonderful gift to me.

By the way, Martin and Cathy are still my dearest of friends and may be coming to visit me next month. There are more vampires around in England and elsewhere. I know of four or five others besides my dear friends Martin and Cathy. Some [ordinary] people know what I am; others do not. Both [types] seem to enjoy it, and one or two have asked me to do it again. The ones who don't know say that I am such a loving friend, and so enjoy it when I give them my special love bite.

Oh, by the way, it's not true about garlic—Martin loves the stuff.

Both of these stories present characteristics attributed to vampires in folklore and fiction. There is an initiation into vampirism that involves the taking of blood or vital energy by the vampire. This is true of folklore vampires; however, their victims become vampires only upon death. In fiction, we find victims who become vampires after being bitten, but remain living in their human bodies.

Kevin's changes incorporate both folklore and literary characteristics. The reputed inability of the vampire to cross running water appears almost universally in folklore and applies not only to vampires, but to all infernal entities and witches as well. This weakness is reiterated in vampire literature. The heightened senses and increased physical strength and stamina are literary inventions that have become so pervasive that they evidently have entered the collective psyche as traits expected of a vampire.

The vampirizing of energy by Judith and Kevin's vampire friend, Mike, is found universally in reports of the living being attacked by the dead or by demons. Judith's reported healing ability and Mike's ability to infuse energy add curious new wrinkles to vampirism, for they are the antithesis of what a vampire traditionally does to others: Vampires take, they do not give. In Judith's case, it is possible that she possessed an innate, but dormant, natural healing ability that was activated by her psychological change. It also is possible that this trait helped to mitigate the supposedly evil nature of the vampire, to make being a vampire more acceptable.

According to Judith, the folklore adage that vampires fear garlic is not true. I encountered other self-professed vampires who agreed, and some who disagreed, claiming that garlic had the power to burn them. The literary vampire has broken away from this folklore remedy against evil as writers have sought to freshen the vampire character. Many modern literary vampires consume garlic without a twinge. So, too, it seems, do some living vampires.

Kevin and Judith present two different views of Vampire Reality. Other self-professed vampires I met had their own unique perspectives.

Chapter Two

Dancing with Satan

IN LONDON, A PAIR OF VAMPIRES FOUND ME.

It was long after midnight one hot summer night that these vampires rang me up in my Paddington flat. At first, I was annoyed. Not because vampires were calling—I didn't know who was on the other end of the line—but because I was being jerked from a much desired sleep.

I picked up the receiver without turning on the light and a machine-gun female voice with a thick northern accent began firing away at me. For several moments I was lost in a hail of verbal bullets as I struggled to keep up with her. (I would not make a good vampire—I am not very lucid after eleven.)

Who? Damien? Right, Damien Vanian, the vampire. Yes, the one Allen J. Gittens, the founder and president of the Vampyre Society in Chippenham had referred to me. Lucidity returned.

Damien informed me that she and her vampire companion, a German named Damon [Damien and

17

Damon are their vampire names], would be happy to get together with me for an interview. They rarely gave interviews; the press could be so insulting, like the time they were featured in a London tabloid that treated them like some freak roadside attraction. But nights in their tiny bedsit flat—a single room in a residential hotel—had grown dull. Most of the fabulous Gothic nightclubs that had once been their playground were long gone, and they and other vampires spent night after night commiserating on the shortage of good entertainment.

We agreed, to my relief, that the vampires would come to my flat for the interview instead of me going to their bedsit. "You'd be disappointed anyway to see how we live," Damien said of their tiny room with a bed, all they could afford on her government dole. Ideally, she preferred to be interviewed after she'd had a chance to fix herself up a bit—her black hair needed to be redyed to cover up the brown roots, her fake nails needed repair, and her artificial fangs were chipped. No self-respecting vampire, she explained, would go out in public without the proper clothes and makeup and everything in good repair.

I assured her that I wouldn't mind a few imperfections. "I'll have some food," I said. "What would you like to eat?"

Peals of laughter sounded on the other end of the line. "She wants to know what I want to *eat*," Damien said to her companion. More laughter. "What do I want to *eat*? Your *neck!*"

"I can't offer you blood," I said hastily. "How about something else to drink?"

Damien said, "No alcohol, luv, but I'll tell you what's the next best thing to blood: Mix orange juice

18

and tomato juice together half and half. It's almost like the real thing. And wait till it *clots*. Mmmmmm!"

Several evenings later, I awaited the vampires' arrival. The refrigerator was stocked with plenty of the prescribed blood substitute. The main entrance to the building was locked at all hours, controlled by round-the-clock desk staff. I thought it best to wait in the lobby and settled in, appropriately, with a copy of Anne Rice's *The Queen of the Damned*.

At about the appointed hour of the vampires' arrival, I noticed the desk woman stiffen. "Are there strange-looking people dressed in black outside?" I asked.

"Two of them," she said, her features frozen in horror.

I smiled. "My guests."

Damien swept in, followed by Damon. They were dressed in full vampire drag: head-to-foot draping black outfits accented with silver crosses, crucifixes, chains, and rings. Their hair was coal black. Damien's thick, long hair was parted in the middle and combed straight, like the Morticia character from Charles Addams's "The Addams Family." Damon's hair was teased up so that it spouted off his head in fountain sprays. They were in whiteface, with black lips and black-ringed eyes. Damien sported pointed nails polished in ruby. When she smiled, her pronounced canines gleamed. I couldn't see the chips in the fangs that she had referred to on the phone, but decided against a close inspection.

Back in the flat, we settled down in my lumpy beige furniture with glasses of my homemade vampire grog. Damon and Damien began chain-smoking. Damien did most of the talking, chattering away in her machine-gun style. Every now and then, Damon would offer some remark or respond to a question, but his style of speech was phlegmatic by comparison to Damien's, and often she would jump in before he completed what he was saying.

We were all in jovial spirits, and as the evening wore on Damien became more and more animated, her speech increasing to such a rapid-fire pace that I could barely keep up with her. We drank every drop of the ersatz blood. Much to my relief, my guests expressed no desire to move on to the real thing. The air became thick and heavy with smoke and the humid heat of the night, and the apartment began to take on bizarre shapes and angles. For the first time since my arrival in London, I was aware of odd shadows pooled in the corners of the living room and in the hallway that led to the bedroom. And when Damien announced with great excitement the entrance of Valan, one of the true Undead whose spirit form was visible only to her and Damon, I half expected him to manifest in the flesh in a puff of smoke.

Damien and Damon live a bare-bones existence on the dole. Damien, thirty-four, and Damon, twenty-four, have been together about four years. They have a three-year-old son, named Valan after the invisible Undead vampire who keeps Damien company, but they profess to live now like brother and sister. Damien said she finds sex repugnant.

Damien has had a hard life from childhood. At age three, she suffered an accident at home that caused her to bleed heavily. She said she blames her father for the accident—that he caused her to run face-first into a vise and cut herself badly. She said she was thrown out of the house at age fourteen. She has never held a steady job and has suffered a variety of medical complaints. She has vertigo, vision problems, and migraines. Sunlight makes her skin blister, she said. She has spent many years at odds with government agencies; nonetheless, she professes to be happy as a vampire and resists the efforts of social workers to change her into a "normal person." She said she believes she has had six past lives as a vampire, which she discovered through hypnosis and dreams. In her most recent past life, she said, she had been guillotined in France on charges of being a witch. She said she could have chosen to be something other than a vampire, but has always opted for this path. She felt she was stuck somehow, perhaps unable to let go of the past.

Damon was born in northern Germany and moved to England at around age twenty. From childhood, he was fascinated with the Gothic movement, punk, and the occult. His family disapproved of his interests. "I've always been an odd type of person, and in Germany it is heavy to be different," he said. "At age twelve I wanted to have as Gothic a room as possible. Eventually I came out on the vampire side." When he came to England, he was a technophobe who could not even use a telephone—most vampires are technophobes, the two agreed. He met Damien, and she drew him more deeply into the vampire's world and taught him how to get along with the telephone and other modern technology. He professes more of an interest in psychic vampirism than in blood-drinking vampirism. Unlike Damien, he can go outside during the day, but too much sunlight hurts him. He spends much of his waking hours in a living dream, he said, dreaming about vampires as he walks down the street. "I think the vampire moves in something that may be another dimension in the dreamtime," he said. "I have to push myself out of the dream world."

I asked, "How can you call yourselves vampires when according to folklore, one must be dead before one can turn into a vampire?"

Damien explained that there are varying degrees of vampirehood, which she described as rungs on a ladder. On the lowest rung are vampirelike people, and on the highest are the true Undead who exist in spirit form. Damien oddly referred to the Undead vampires as "dead" ones, perhaps because they exist only in nonphysical form. Most vampires come from middle-class backgrounds and "upset" families, she said.

"The first thing we've got to get straight is that every vampire interviewed is going to have a different story," Damien said. "So I'm going to speak only about myself. You've got to be dead to be a vampire, that's obvious. The question is, are you dead? I'd reverse the question. The idea of being a vampire is you don't want to die. They're called 'the living dead,' they're not called 'the dead.' So if you ask me about being dead, it's a little off-putting, because the whole idea of being a vampire is to live for eternity. I don't want to die. Living's the main thing, not dying.

"I do class myself as a vampire. It started when I was about three years old. It was because of blood. I was in a bad accident and I tasted a lot of my own blood. You talk to most vampires, and blood is involved in getting them started. I don't think I've ever come across one where blood hasn't been involved. Vampirelike people watch "The Addams

Family" and "The Munsters" and dress like the characters. There's nothing wrong with that. You can call yourself a vampire if you just dress as a vampire. It's one step up the ladder."

"If the object is to gain eternal life as a vampire, how do you accomplish that while you're living?" I asked.

Damien shrugged. "One doesn't know and one never will. It's a hope, as in any religion. I don't want to go to heaven, so there's only one other place to go and that's hell. It's obviously the better of the two. As for me, I'm better off than most vampires. Mine's quite a strange story. You see, I am in contact with a real vampire, Valan. I actually see him. Valan came to me the day I had the accident when I was three and he's stayed with me ever since. When I was growing up, I was told he was an imaginary friend. He's still here. I'm aware of him almost all the time, but I can't *bring* him into a room. I find it's getting harder to actually see Valan as I'm getting older. A clairvoyant I know says Valan is on a different plane. We keep each other alive, more or less. The idea is for me to get Valan into a form down here on earth so that he can eventually get me to where he is, so I can be a real vampire. We're not actually going to trade places. It's hard to explain. The thing is, I may be very old by the time this happens. There's a chance I could die first, but there's more hope for me for eternal life than for some other vampires. Valan is doing this for me."

"What does Valan look like?"

Damien gave me a sly smile. "I find him very attractive. Beauty is in the eye of the beholder. Valan is very aristocratic, the type that people expect aristocrats to be. He tends to go for pink ribbons."

"He puts pink ribbons on everything," chimed in Damon, "Sometimes he covers items in pink ribbons, like parcels. Another thing, he can move small items from one place to another."

Damon said he can also see the Undead vampire from time to time. Once in Germany, he was in a graveyard with a friend. Damien was not with them, but both Damon and his friend saw Valan jump up and down amidst the graves. "Playing funny fellow," Damon said.

"I don't know how it works," Damien added. "Valan has got more answers than I could ever have questions. I'm just following the dead vampires."

"Has he told you about himself, where he comes from and how he got to be a vampire?"

"Yeah, he has, but I don't want to talk about it. He can't speak for himself, and I don't want to upset him or say something out of order. I find it easier to talk about him if there's a psychic in the room. Valan is why I'm not pulling out of being a vampire, even though there's too much seriousness around the vampire now. The vampires are all morbid. It should be more fun. But call yourself a vampire and see how people react to you. Most people start giving you a hard time. The real thing about the vampire is, you don't want burying. My God, you don't want burying. Who wants to be six foot under the ground? *I* don't."

Damien then acknowledged that Valan has an Undead brother, Darren, whom she also sees occasionally. "Nobody else seems to see Darren or want to talk about him. Some clairvoyants I've been to have mentioned Darren, but they won't deal with him. He's a bit more vampiric inside than Valan is. Valan is the type who wouldn't frighten people because he looks like what they expect from the films. But Darren is not the prettiest person in the world. If either Valan or Darren gets weaker, the other gets stronger. If somebody really hurt me, I should imagine Darren would slap them. He has done it, actually. I can't say, 'Oh, God, I'm in trouble, Darren, help me,' and get results. But there have been cases when I've been in real trouble and he has slapped people around."

"Have any other people seen Valan?" I asked.

"Damon had a friend in Germany who didn't believe in ghouls or vampires," Damien said. "The friend came out one day and said to Damon, 'Who's that guy Damien keeps talking to?' Damon said, 'What does he look like?' The friend explained quite thoroughly what he looked like, what clothes he wore. He saw him as real as we are talking to you. But there was nobody standing there.

"A psychiatrist actually saw him, too. I'd gone into his office, and he said, 'Would you mind removing that idiot with the long black hair out of the room?' I said, 'You mean *him?*' I could see Valan, too. He said, 'Yeah, him.' I said, 'Come on, Valan, let's move out of here.' And I got up and left."

According to Damien, there are many more true Undead like Valan and Darren than most people would like to believe. "We're working with the dead ones through rituals," she said. "We're ranked through the dead ones. Damon is very low on the ladder. I'm purple—that's one below top. The more you obey the dead ones, the higher you go. You don't give all the secrets away, either. You know when to talk and when to shut up."

Damien said she believes vampires are the children of Satan. "God was supposed to create the earth.

Satan created all the vampires. I really do believe that," she told me.

I asked her why, when many other self-professed vampires go to great lengths to dissociate themselves from Satan.

"It's my point of view. I'm quite strong on that one. I can see what the other vampires are saying: They're undead, they don't go to heaven and they don't go to hell. But I've actually met Satan. I know which side *my* bread is buttered on. There's two choices: up or down."

"You met Satan? How?"

Damien became uneasy. "I frighten myself so much if I talk about it. It's so frightening to find that you've got no power over yourself at all. Satan is the most beautiful being I've ever seen. I'm not a satanist, by the way. I've seen him on three occasions. Being a vampire, I can't go into that. I've frightened myself so bad on that."

I pressed her for details about her encounters with Satan, but it was the one subject she refused to elaborate on. The marked change in her voice and body language clearly expressed how much the experiences had frightened her.

To ease her discomfort, I changed the subject. "Tell me about your lifestyle."

Damien gave an odd answer. "I have terrible dreams. When I go to sleep, I dream for hours and I don't wake up. That's why Damon stays with our son Valan, you see. Valan has asthma and if he gets sick or something, I can't be woken up. Once my head hits that pillow, that's it. I go to bed about six in the morning and get up about three in the afternoon. And nobody's ever going to change that. It means I can't get jobs. I don't care. There's nothing they can do about that. I've had jobs in hotels and have done really well, but you always get one person who comes in and destroys it, a Christian or whatever. I'm not against Christians. I'm not really interested in anybody's religion at all. I don't go around trying to do anything to anybody else."

"Are you part of a group?"

"No. There aren't many. There is, it is said, a large group of vampires in Hastings. I've never met them. But any time you get a group, you start getting wrong things like with the Christians. I always work on my own. I don't get up in the morning and say, 'I'm a vampire.' I get up at three o'clock in the afternoon and I get on with my life like anybody else does. I have to. I don't think about being a vampire until I hit the street. Then most people think I'm just a Gothic, so it's not too much of a problem."

"You mentioned that you're always at risk of some-one 'destroying' your life," I said. "What do you mean?"

"You have problems with the law," said Damon.

"If you have children and you're a vampire, watch out," said Damien. She explained that about ten years earlier, she had borne a daughter out of wedlock and was forced to give her up for adoption because of her life as a vampire. She said that she and Damon periodically are visited by social workers who investigate their lifestyle. The social workers come because suspicious neighbors report them to the authorities, she said. She added that in the past she has been prevented from moving, forbidden to wear black for a period of two years, and forced to cut her below-waist-length hair.

"I'm not feeling sorry for myself," she said. "If you've got a child and you're in a different religion than Christianity in this country, if you're poor and you can't say you're a family unit, you're a prime target. The vampires I know won't have children for that particular reason. It's too much stress.

"I had my daughter and I had to put her down for adoption because I was living on only four pounds sixty a week and had nowhere to live. The father was actually a *therapist* for vampires. I'd gone to him for *help.*" Damien laughed sarcastically. "I'm not into sex, so I'm sure I was 'fiddled.' He was a hypnotist. He was supposed to be an expert on vampires. Some expert! So when I got to the hospital to have the baby, I had to put her down for adoption. I was told that if I wanted to keep her, they wanted to analyze what I actually was—was I a vampire because I had a blood disorder, maybe? I thought, For my daughter's sake, let it be a blood disorder. I don't like needles, but I let them take one blood sample. They came back and said they had to pull twenty. I said, 'No, bullshit, and I'm off. I'm *taking* blood, I'm not giving it.' I was a little frightened that if they found a blood disorder and cured it, I would become normal. I don't want to change. You see, most people are frightened of being vampires and they want changing. The social workers don't have anybody like me saying they don't want changing."

After giving up her daughter, Damien remained under the auspices of social services. "I was referred to a social worker who was supposed to help me get accommodations. I went through four years of hell. You can't change social workers. I was accused of being mad. They'll have words with you like that in their offices. I was put into an institution. I was told I could leave anytime, but the second I tried to leave, they said, 'No, there's no way you can leave.' So I was held without my consent. The police actually stood up for me and said, 'You can't keep her, she hasn't done anything wrong.' But they said, 'No, we're putting her on an order.' But what can they do? If you don't want changing, there's nothing they can do.

"Well, they can only hold you without consent for six months at a time. I was enjoying myself. There was a bed, radio, television set, food every day. I didn't have to go looking for it. So they threw me out in the end. They said I was enjoying myself far too much." Damien laughed at the irony.

After she lost her daughter and was removed from the institution, Damien fell into a depression. She had no money and nowhere to live. She tried twice to commit suicide by overdosing on drugs. She wanted to demonstrate to the authorities that she would rather die than stop being a vampire, she said. She later learned how the dole system worked and was able to obtain funds. Then, around 1982, she was suddenly denied money.

"I went to the dole office and they told me I was officially dead! I couldn't get my dole. They made a big joke out of it. It didn't get straightened out for a long time. I had to get a new national insurance number. Until it got straightened out, I had to live in a graveyard for three years."

"How did you live in a graveyard?"

Damien shrugged. "You have a suitcase and you just make the best of what you can. I had to wash in the cold taps. There were a few others living in there as well—two gay vampires. It was Brompton Cemetery. I slept in the vaults. I didn't touch any of the coffins—that's illegal. It's quite frightening because the coffins fall down off their shelves sometimes. I had one fall down and I was injured. Obviously, I couldn't go to the hospital and say a coffin fell down on me. The lid actually hit me and I thought, My God, I've had it. They're heavy. If it had fallen flat straight onto me, I wouldn't be here right now. It slid off the shelf and was a crumbling mess. But you can't live in the graveyards now—they're shut down at night and patrolled."

Damon offered the opinion that vampires have an easier time with authorities in Germany. "Laws are very strict and the authorities can't touch you. You can get your way out of troubles. In Germany, if the police get called, they can only inquire about the subject of the complaint—for example, if someone thought you had drugs. Well, we don't take drugs, we don't drink alcohol very often—we only smoke a hell of a lot of cigarettes. Here, if a social worker inquires, they can poke their nose into all kinds of things that don't have to do with the complaint."

"How have you managed to keep your son?" I asked.

Damien said that when she became pregnant with Valan, she and Damon decided to move to Germany, where they expected to find better housing and not to be harassed by the authorities after the baby was born. They were wrong.

"For a while it was quite good," said Damon. "We didn't have the social workers right away when the child was born, which would have been quite dangerous. But then we started to have problems with the neighbors and the people on the street—and my grandmother."

After Valan was born, the vampires left a house they had been renting and moved in with Damon's family. His grandmother took a dislike to Damien. "The police were called on several occasions," Damien said. "They told me I had to get out of the house. A clairvoyant friend told me I had three hours to get out of the house and get out of Germany or I was dead. So I packed a bag and we came back over here.

"Then police came around, the social workers came around, and it took me a hell of a lot of effort to keep my son. It was through sheer luck that Damon was with me. They seemed to trust Damon and said if he stayed with me, fine, I could keep my son."

"It's taken us two or three years to fight the authorities," put in Damon. "We've gone through three social workers."

"I sit at home waiting for the next call," said Damien. "It never finishes. My case has been closed at least three times now. Then somebody else calls the authorities and you have to move to a different area. Somebody else calls and you move to a different flat. The cycle starts again. You're never ever safe."

"Is your son a vampire?" I asked.

"The authorities say he decides for himself what he wants to be," Damien said. "Valan has a real sense of humor. I told him he's not a real vampire yet. We call him a kissing vampire because he's got a strange habit of kissing your eye sockets out. He's got it wrong, but there's no way you can tell him it's either the lips or the leg. No, he's got to suck your eye socket out. You'll be fast asleep in bed and he'll go, 'The kissing vampire is here!' He's a very strong person. It won't matter if he grows up to be a vampire, a vicar or a priest, or whatever. We don't make him wear black. He gets to choose any color he wants. We take him shopping and he tends to stick to red and blue. He likes some black. They [the authorities] told me I couldn't have a coffin to sleep in because he might think I'm a vampire, and I would be in big trouble. I'm sitting there clacking my fangs. How on earth is that going to make a difference? I would *love* a coffin. I don't want to spend my whole life hiding anymore. They've already tried to frighten me, terrorize me, take the kid. If they're going to do it, they will. I'm not allowed to have a black room, either. There's no law says I can't, but if I do, the authorities are going to inquire."

In addition to feeling threatened by government agencies, the London vampires feel threatened on the streets. They said they seldom go out in public because of harassment. "We walk down the street and get all this abuse," said Damien, explaining that their vampire clothing is a magnet for attention.

Despite the stares and heckling it draws, neither one would ever consider leaving the flat dressed as an ordinary human being—it wouldn't be fitting for a proper vampire. "We sit on the tube [London Underground Transportation] and we're the ones being attacked, which in the modern day I find very strange," she said. "It's supposed to be the other way around! But you get some brainless shit in a big car with a T-shirt on and there's no dealing with him. Most of the people who pass you on the street will either laugh or smile. But you don't know which one will attack. What can you do? You can't do anything. I usually keep it light—you know, where's the masquerade ball, where's the hearse, can't get a hearse driver anywhere. But you only need one person to destroy that. You go out and you think, 'Right! World, here I come. *Move!*' And somebody calls you an idiot and all your power seems to go *blop*. It's the one thing that frightens us, so we won't go out. My nerves are terrible. I'm not surprised, with what's been going on over the years."

"In Germany, the people, the peasants, are running around wild and can give you a lot of trouble," said Damon. "They are very unfriendly toward vampires. I was beaten up in Germany three times because of my appearance. After that my confidence dropped."

"Yeah, your confidence drops *very* fast," Damien agreed.

Damon went on. "I got more and more troubled. It's taken me a long time to get over this fear."

"A lot of us vampires are afraid to go out," said Damien. "That seems really strange. But we're too frightened. The thing is, I'm an A-grade coward. I see people who say they're going to be vampires into the next century, they're never going to change, but within months or years, as soon as the trouble starts, you can't find them. I saw this happen in 1971 when vampires came out in public. I saw it again in 1976 when the punks came out. I saw it again in 1982 when the Goths came out. You can walk around London now and you can't find *anybody*. The thing is, I can't change. And *I'm* still here."

Damon observed, "We live in a society where we are the odd ones out."

Damien shrugged. "There's hard times, there's good times. You get that everywhere. I used to go to nightclubs every night and really enjoy myself. That's what it's all about. Everyone had a club name, you never knew any real names, and there were no questions asked, anything was hip. But there's too much aggression now. You can't go out and enjoy yourself."

Damon pointed to one of his earrings, a huge silver crucifix dangling upside down from his left earlobe. It had been left at his doorstep by a self-professed enemy of vampires, apparently in the hopes of preventing him from entering his home. Damon chuckled as he explained how he had taken it to a jeweler and had it turned into an earring. "I'm not afraid of crosses," he said, "but I am frightened of garlic. A lot of vampires cannot go near garlic because if they eat garlic, it makes them physically sick. The crosses I don't fear. But the garlic does actually affect me. If I'm eating something at someone's house and my mouth starts to blister and burn, then I know I've eaten garlic."

"How can you be frightened of other people?" I asked. "As vampires, don't you have any supernormal powers?"

Damien said this was not so. "The old vampires, the dead ones that have the supernatural powers, did they have the powers before they were dead or did they get them after? If they got them after, then they were like us. They can't all have been supernatural before they died. People are slamming us down because we're not like them. Maybe in another ten, twenty, thirty years we'll be doing the same thing."

What Damien and Damon had to say on the subject of blood was surprising: Self-professed vampires cannot consume much blood.

"Once you've tasted blood, you know there is some sort of power behind it," Damien said. "You should be able to step up the ladder one step farther. In the beginning, drinking blood into the gullet is going to make you sick like alcohol or smoking. But like any sort of drug, you're going to keep going back for more. There is a feeling of power when you drink it. The one thing I've learned over the years is that if you keep drinking blood in large amounts into the gullet, it can kill you. I've seen vampires who drink blood out of glasses. It can cause throat infections. It might have worms in it and can cause bad vomiting. It can cause death in the end, if you drink it in large amounts. This is what a few vampires don't really know, that you can kill yourself by drinking large amounts of blood. One drink, in some cases, can last you right through to the grave. You get vampires who try to do it as a trend and drink it every week, but you don't need to do that. My motto is, a few drops will suffice.

"The original vampires didn't take it orally. They had holes in the bottoms of the teeth and used them like siphons, which in the modern day is like a blood transfusion. There's one vampire I know who does a blood transfusion quite regularly. That's the way it should be done properly. You get younger and fresher blood coming through. I'm waiting for a proper blood transfusion myself. We've not got the money together yet to do it. It can be done, but if you say that publicly, the hospitals will ring up and say they don't do it, they've never heard of it. You don't have to pay for it, really, you just wait until you've had a bad accident."

"Until you can get a transfusion, how do you consume blood?"

"Here we go again," said Damien with a trace of exasperation. "Like I said, you don't need it that often, though you do get vampires who will need it. Once you taste blood and you get this knowledge from it, then you don't need to drink it all the time. It's an individual thing and difficult to explain. I don't need it that often. I can drink blood every five years. I used to get blood from the butcher shop. I drained it off all the meat trays. But the doctor told me that I was getting a throat infection and I've got to watch it."

"The last time I drank blood was four years ago," said Damon. "Again, from the butcher shops."

Damien seemed vexed that other people expect her to have a craving for blood because she is a vampire. "I was in a restaurant with two vampires. I ordered my steak well-done and started a controversy. The waitress had a go at me. But why do I have to eat my meat raw?

"The blood-drinking is secondary to being a vampire," she went on. "You've got people who drink blood who are sadistic. They're not vampires. Even as a vampire, you don't have to drink blood. The sooner somebody dresses like and calls himself a vampire, he's on the right ladder. It doesn't matter how low down on the ladder you are. Once you're dressed in black, once you've got your cape, you're on your way. In magazines, you see people say, 'Oh, I want to be a vampire.' They've got a long way to go. I'm not breaking my fangs on their leg—it's not worth it. Why don't they start to dress as a vampire, see what it feels like? I get so angry, they all sit there saying, 'I'm waiting for a vampire to bite me.' They're waiting for the odd vampire of passion to bite them. In *this* country, they've got a long wait!"

Damien reports that vampires also are confronted by the problem that faces all mortals: aging. She said she is using an increasing amount of cosmetics to try to hide the march of time. "I've aged very quickly because of the situations I've gotten in," she said. "I've gone through such bad times and it's actually ripped the insides of me out, causing a lot of damage and a lot of strain on me."

Vampires, she said, "age by sections of nine years—that's what Satan gives you. I'll look like this for another nine."

"I'm now the age I want to be," said Damon, referring to his twenty-four years. "So now I'm going to be like Damien, struggling and putting more make-up on, creams, trying to keep the aging down."

"I don't think that age is comforting, that it's more knowledge," said Damien. "I've got no vision of me being much older. Maybe another five years, and then I don't know what the hell I'm going to do. Cosmetic surgery, probably."

"I thought consuming blood was supposed to keep vampires young," I said.

Damien nodded. "That's right, it will."

"So why not drink just a little more blood?"

"You're in that vicious circle again. Because drinking blood into the gullet will give you only so much time. You'd have to drink tons of it and then you'd be sick. I will transfuse in the end because my choices will be nil. There are problems—there are problems in anything. But I'm still here and I wouldn't change it for the world. All you've got to do is take a walk out there and take one look at a human being and your power is back again. Valan comes for me—I don't have to worry too much about what I drink. The other vampires, they have to drink the blood to get their eternal youth. I'm hoping that Valan will do that for me. I'm taking the left-hand-left-hand route instead of the straight left."

With all this talk about vampires and Valan, I probably shouldn't have been surprised when Valan the Undead elected to drop in on us. Both Damien and Damon said they could see him, flashing about the room, first here, then there. "Can you see him? Can you see him?" Damien asked excitedly.

I couldn't see a thing. I didn't *want* to see a thing. I wanted Valan, if indeed there was a Valan, to stay in his own plane and not invade mine.

Valan proved to be a good sport. He remained in a reality perceived only by his protégés. And when the vampires took their leave of my flat, they took Valan with them. All that remained were the stale smoke and stubs of countless cigarettes, the dirty glasses empty of vampire grog, and the tapes of the interview with the vampires.

Damien and Damon seemed to fit some of my criteria for being "real" vampires. Although they themselves did not appear to be supernatural in any way, their Vampire Reality involved extrasensory perception of disembodied vampire beings, and in Damien's case, of Satan. A skeptic would call these visions hallucinations produced by the mind, even though they were also seen by others. Yet, too little is known about extrasensory perception and the nature of consciousness to dismiss them outright as such.

But are they truly external beings? Damien stated that Valan had characteristics of literary vampires. She did not offer a description of Satan, but it is likely that her perception of him also was influenced by popular treatment of the Devil in film and fiction, as well as by impressions residing in the collective unconscious. These impressions would include the accumulation of two thousand years of Christian thoughts about the Devil, as well as much older and broader thoughts, encompassing all of humanity, about the personifications of evil.

There are no answers, but we should be open to the possibility that beings exist in other realities, and that on occasion they can enter our reality. However, our perception of them—even our ability to perceive them at all—may be influenced in ways we cannot grasp by forces and material residing deep within our own psyches.

Chapter Three

Will the Real Vampire Please Stand Up

THUS FAR, SEVERAL SELF-PROFESSED VAMPIRES HAVE GIVEN divergent accounts of what it is to be a vampire. If they are not "real" vampires, they are at least living embodiments of collective beliefs about vampires, for as Damien so aptly put it, one technically must be dead in order to be a vampire—according to lore, that is.

But trying to pin down "real" vampires is no easy task, as was noted in Chapter One. Montague Summers (1880–1948), a Catholic theologian and author of a number of books on the infernal, including witchcraft and vampires, states in his now classic works *The Vampire: His Kith and Kin* (1928) and *The Vampire in Europe* (1929) that vampires by definition are dead and must have a physical form. But Summers, like other researchers who believed in the corporeal reality of vampires, never satisfactorily explained how a physical form—the corpse—manages to escape from a grave in order to wander about at night. My own theory is that the vampire who returns from the dead does not have corporeal reality and never did. However, that the returning dead have often *appeared* corporeal to percipients. This is a universal and not unusual phenomenon—there are many reports of ghosts who seem to be solid flesh and blood. Because they seem real, they are believed to be literally reanimated corpses.

Summers also says that noncorporeal entities that assault the living are not truly vampires but are members of the "vampire family." He includes in this category virtually any account of the dead attacking the living. The belief in the ability of the dead to return to the living is ancient and universal, as the returning dead have been blamed for plagues and illness, death and misfortune. Universal remedies to prevent or stop these calamities from happening include nailing the corpse to the coffin, staking it through the heart (almost universally held to be the seat of the soul, and thus the spirit), severing the head and limbs, and burning the corpse. It is a mistake, however, to classify all accounts of the returning dead as vampires, and to disqualify the noncorporeal as vampires.

Perhaps we can gain a better understanding of vampires if we examine the folklore origins of the vampire, and even the history of the word *vampire*. While vampire creatures, demons, and spirits exist universally in folklore and mythology, the vampire that has entered the Western collective unconscious has evolved from the Slavic vampire cult of Eastern Europe. It was not until the eighteenth century that our modern concept of the vampire began to take shape.

Historic Origins of the Vampire

Vampire is a borrowed term, coming into the English language for the first time in 1732, when a newspaper translated a French account of an Austrian surgeon's report in German of a vampire epidemic in Austrian-occupied Serbia. The term thus twisted its way from Serbian into English.

The Serbian term from which *vampire* was borrowed is *vampir*. But it is much more complicated than that because *vampir* is equated with numerous other Slavic terms, such as *lampir, varcolaci, pricolici, vukodlak, vapir, vepir, upir,* and *ala*. All of these words have shades of meaning that today's *Websters* wouldn't recognize as *vampire*, according to the definition given in Chapter One.

The ancient Slavs originated in the region of Europe north of the Carpathian Mountains between the Vistula and Dnieper rivers. Little is known about them, except that they evidently were sun worshipers and were heavily influenced by the beliefs of the Persians, to whom they were closely related. Scholars theorize that the ancient Slavs may have first considered the vampire to be a demonic creature who sucked up storm and rain clouds.

Beginning in the fifth century AD, the Slavs pushed out of their homeland, moving south to the Balkan peninsula, north into Russia, and west along the Elbe River. This migration lasted until about the ninth century, when the Slavs were absorbed into the Christian West.

For centuries, Christianity existed alongside earlier religious beliefs and mythologies. Other religious influences on the Slavs were Mithraism, a Persian cult, and Manichaeism and Bogomilism, both of which espoused dualism that held that there are two forces in the cosmos, Good (often identified with spirit and soul) and Evil (matter and body). The demonology of the Bogomils included belief in demons that could lead humans into wickedness and after death dwell in their corpses and await resurrection, when both would be punished.

The Bogomils considered the dead to belong to the Forces of Destruction (Evil) and had strict procedures for disposing of bodies. Corpses were not to be brought into church or attended by priests, but taken straight to the place of burial. Women, relatives of the dead, and minors were forbidden to be present at burial, and no mourning was allowed. Relatives of the dead were to visit the grave on the third and fortieth days after burial and offer prayers so that the soul of the deceased would be resettled in the body of a newborn person.

Thus the seeds of the vampire cult were planted— the concept that after death a corpse might be so afflicted with evil that it would leave the grave to attack the living.

The Slavic vampire cult coalesced in about the fifteenth century. The cult varied from village to village. The basic principles, though, remained fairly constant: The dead (now part of the earth and the forces of Evil) could under certain circumstances rise up and attack the living, draining away strength, vitality, and life. They could be fought with the forces of Good, such as light and fire, and by piercing the heart and cutting off the head of the corpse, which contained the soul. Within this framework, different villages developed their own unique methods of dealing with this evil.

The vampire cult was not discovered by the West until the eighteenth century. When Austria conquered Serbia, its soldiers encountered case after case in remote villages of corpses being exhumed from their graves and mutilated or cremated in order to rid the village of nocturnal afflictions—alleged attacks by the dead—and of diseases believed to be caused by the restless dead. In 1732, Austrian Army Surgeon Johann Fluckinger wrote a report on a virtual epidemic of vampires in Serbia, thus lighting a veritable bonfire of Western fascination with and outrage at such heathen practices. Numerous studies quickly followed, including the now-famous one by Dom Calmet, a French theologian.

The investigators encountered a host of beliefs. Vampires were variously believed to be living persons, reanimated corpses, and spirits of the disturbed dead. Terms were applied to beings that sometimes were reanimated corpses and other times were creatures that ate the sun and moon, similar to those in other mythologies who are credited with causing eclipses. Such sun-eating and moon-eating creatures were, variously, animals smaller than dogs, dragons, or octopus-like sucking beings.

Some of the vampire creatures were believed to have the power to shape-shift from human into animal form. The *obur* of the Karachay people was a person who acted similarly to the alleged witches hunted down by Christian authorities during the Middle Ages and Renaissance. The *obur* would smear itself with magical salve, mount a broom and rise up the chimney in the form of a cat, enter a home by descending the chimney, drink the blood of sleeping children, attack livestock and drink animal blood, and then shape-shift back into human form.

The Hag and the Vampire

Folklore also relates vampires to demonic beings such as the poltergeist and *mara*. The poltergeist—from a German term meaning "noisy spirit"—plagues humans with physical assaults of pinching and biting and moves objects about, while the *mara* attacks sleeping humans and sexually assaults them. These in turn have association with the hag syndrome, also called the old hag.

Characteristics of the hag syndrome vary somewhat, but all accounts include the same basic element. If you were to have a hag attack, it probably would unfold like this:

You are awakened from sleep by the sound of soft footfalls in the dark. Someone—or *something*—is approaching your bed. Your heart pounds and you lie motionless on your back, straining to see into the dark yet terrified of what might be revealed. You see nothing. The footfalls come closer. They sound like shoes being dragged across velvet. Slow. Deliberate.

You sense a presence but still see nothing. Your chest

45

aches. You sweat. The presence takes on a tangible feel. It looms closer, an ink stain barely perceptible in the night. It emanates energy. The energy is *evil*. A disgusting smell fills the air.

Suddenly you are pressed into the bed by an enormous weight upon your chest. The air is slammed from your lungs, and the weight is so heavy you can scarcely take new air in. You feel you are suffocating. You try to struggle, to scream out, but your limbs are paralyzed and the scream strangles in your throat. You see a shape on top of you, and my God, *it isn't human!* Two red eyes glare at you. You are wild with fear that this *thing* is going to kill you. And you are powerless to save yourself or summon help.

Abruptly and without warning, just as you think you're going to pass out or die, the attack ends. The thing with its red eyes vanishes. You draw in great draughts of air. For some time, you are afraid to move, lest your movements summon the creature to descend once again and finish you off. You feel exhausted. Nothing happens. The night is still and silent. When you feel confident enough, you turn on a light, rise, and inspect the house. Nothing is amiss. You return to bed. Still shaky, you cannot sleep. You stay awake the rest of the night, on your guard against the return of the thing.

The hag syndrome has been recorded since ancient times. The second-century Greek physician Galen wrote about it, and chalked it up to indigestion. Gastric disturbances might indeed cause unsettled dreams, but many a hag victim has been attacked on an empty stomach.

Victims may sleep at night or nap during the day. They almost always sleep on their backs. They may hear footsteps, feel and see a form, and smell odors, or they may simply wake up suddenly, feeling an invisible, crushing weight and paralysis, followed by cessation and exhaustion. Regardless of the characteristics, the attacks are always terrifying. In his book *The Terror That Comes in the Night* (1982), folklorist David J. Hufford estimated that about 15 percent of the general population worldwide suffers at least one hag attack. Some individuals had suffered attacks several times a year. Rarely were individuals subjected to frequent attacks over a limited period of time. Even rarer were those who suffered frequent and chronic attacks. Belief in the hag or the supernatural in general, and previous supernatural experiences, did not seem to be factors in whether or not an individual had a hag attack—even the most hard-boiled skeptic has been vulnerable.

No adequate explanation for the hag has been put forward. Poor circulation, indigestion, witchcraft, demons, and vampires have all been blamed throughout history. In folklore, hags were sometimes described as supernatural creatures that acted on their own volition, or who were directed to attack a person through magic. They were associated with, but not equated with, incubi and succubi. (The latter are male and female demons, respectively, that are said to sexually assault human beings, especially in their sleep.) Hag attacks have been characterized by crushing weight and terror, but not sexual assault.

Hags also were described as witches, sorcerers, and practitioners of magic who traveled out of their bodies to attack other human beings in spirit form, riding their chests at night. The term *hag* was often used to refer to a witch, and to be *hagged* or *hagridden* meant one had been assaulted by a witch in spirit form at night.

Ernest Jones, an influential psychoanalyst of the Freudian school, equated hag attacks with nightmares in his classic monograph *On the Nightmare* (1931). Jones attributed nightmares to sexual repression. He noted that the term *nightmare* came from the Anglo-Saxon terms *neaht* or *nicht* (night) and *mara* (incubus or succubus, literally "the crusher"). Up until the mid-seventeenth century, the term *nightmare* was used to describe these types of nocturnal attacks. Jones considered vampires and werewolves to be expressions of repressed sexuality as well.

Today, Jones's viewpoint seems restrictive and outdated. Sexual repression may be a factor in some hag cases, but it is too sweeping to attribute all cases to such a cause. Likewise, sleep-related illnesses such as narcolepsy may be a factor in some cases, but cannot account for all or even a majority of them.

Supernatural factors cannot be ruled out. As Hufford found, the hag syndrome has played a significant role in the development of various supernatural traditions, and therefore the hag's relationship to cultural factors deserves more investigation.

Anecdotal material has linked the hag to the vampire. Montague Summers, in his book *The Vampire in Europe,* cites some vampire cases that have some of the characteristics of the hag attack. Reports of the malevolent dead molesting the living at night survive from twelfth-century England. It was believed that the Devil reanimated their corpses. The suspected corpses were exhumed; some disgorged blood. They were burned according to the traditional method of dispatching evil. Another example Summers presents is taken from philosopher Henry More's work *An Antidote against Atheism: or, An Appeal to the Natural Faculties of the Mind of Man, Whether There Be Not a God* (1653).

The case is that of an unnamed shoemaker in Silesia who on September 20, 1591, took his shoemaker's knife and slit his own throat in the garden of his home. To avoid the disgrace and taint of the sin of suicide, the family announced that he had died of apoplexy. They washed and wrapped the corpse so artfully that the parson and others were fooled, and the man was given a Christian burial. Within six weeks, however, rumors began to circulate among the townsfolk that the shoemaker had in truth taken his own life. The town officials were prodded to dig up the corpse and examine it. The widow confessed the truth to the town council, but managed to persuade them to leave the body in the ground, claiming it would serve no good purpose to give in to the rumormongers. Summers wrote:

> But while these things are in agitation, to the astonishment of the Inhabitants of the place, there appears a *Spectrum* in the exact shape and habit of the deceased, and that not only at night, but at mid-day. Those that were asleep it terrified with horrible visions; those that were waking it would strike, pull or press, lying heavy upon them like an *Ephialtes:* so that there were perpetual complaints every morning of their last night's rest through the whole Town. . . .
>
> For no sooner did the Sun hide his head, but this *Spectrum* would be sure to appear, so that every body was fain to look about him, and stand upon his guard, which was a sore trouble to those whom the Labours of the Day made more sensible of the want of rest in the night. For this terrible *Apparrition* [sic] would sometimes stand by their bed-sides, sometimes cast itself upon the midst of their beds, would lie close to them, would miserably suffocate them, and would strike them and pinch them, that not only blue marks, but plain impressions of his fingers would be upon sundry parts

of their bodies in the morning. Nay, such was the violence and impetuousness of this Ghost, that when men forsook their beds, and kept their dining-rooms, with Candles lighted, and many of them in company together, the better to secure themselves from fear and disturbance; yet he would then appear to them and have a bout with some of them, notwithstanding all this provision against it.

The aggrieved townsfolk finally prevailed upon the authorities to dig up the shoemaker's corpse. The job was done on April 18, 1592. They were shocked to find that:

> His body was found entire, not at all putrid, no ill smell about him, saving the mustiness of the Grave-cloaths, his joints limber and flexible, as in those that are alive, his skin only flaccid, but a more fresh grown in the room of it, the wound of his throat gaping, but no gear nor corruption in it; there was also observed a Magical mark in the great toe of his right foot, *viz.* an Excrescency in the form of a Rose.

The shoemaker's corpse was kept out of the earth until April 24, then reburied under a gallows in a superstitious attempt to appease the unquiet spirit. The attacks on the living not only continued, they expanded to include the dead man's family.

> Wherefore the seventh of *May* he was again digged up, and it was observable, that he was grown more sensibly fleshy since his last interment. To be short, they cut off the Head, Arms, and Legs of the Corps, and opening his Back, took out his Heart, which was as fresh and intire [*sic*] as in a Calf new kill'd. These, together with his Body, they put on a pile of wood, and burnt them to Ashes, which they carefully sweeping

together, and putting into a Sack (that none might get them for wicked uses) poured them into the River, after which the *Spectrum* was never seen more.

The shoemaker's maid, who died after him, also returned and assaulted a fellow servant at night, lying on the woman so heavily that her eyes swelled. The spirit appeared also in the forms of a hen, a cat, and a goat, and bedeviled others to the point where the maid's body was disinterred and burned. The attacks ceased.

Still another haglike vampire case was reported in the 1730s in the Serbian village of Medvegia (also given as Meduegna). According to the records of investigating medical officers, a woman named Stanacka (also recorded as Stana) "lay down to sleep fifteen days ago, fresh and healthy, but at midnight started up out of her sleep with a terrible cry, fearful and trembling, and complained that she had been throttled by the son of a haiduk by the name of Milloe [or Milloc], who had died nine weeks earlier, whereupon she had experienced a great pain in the chest and became worse by the hour, until finally she died on the third day." In Montague Summers's account of the case, as given in *The Vampire in Europe,* Stana (as he gave the woman's name) confessed on her deathbed that she had "anointed herself in the blood of a vampire to liberate herself from his persecutions." Her baby died, too. When vampire hunters dug up the woman's body, they found it, said Summers, "untouched by decomposition. When it was opened the chest was found to be full of fresh blood, the viscera had all the appearance of sound health. The skin and nails of both hands and feet were loose and came off, but underneath was a clean new skin and nails." The body of her baby also was exhumed, but had been so savaged by wolves that too little was left of it to determine if vampirism was present. The body of Milloe, or Milloc, was dug up after the sixteen-year-old boy had lain in the grave for ninety days. Said Summers, "It was rosy and flabber, wholly in the Vampire condition."

In addition to hag characteristics, both cases had characteristics of poltergeist attacks and hauntings by revenants, which are spirits of the dead who walk the earth. The shoemaker's case had further vampire characteristics, in the depletion of energy of the living, and the uncorrupted corpse. The latter was considered a certain sign that he had turned into a vampire.

Summers also cites a later case, published in the *Occult Review* in 1924, researched by the occultist Dr. Franz Hartmann. It is, states Summers, among the "typical instances of vampirism." It also strongly resembles the hag encounter:

A miller at D—— had a healthy servant-boy, who soon after entering his service began to fail. He acquired a ravenous appetite, but nevertheless grew daily more feeble and emaciated. Being interrogated, he at last confessed that a thing which he could not see, but which he could plainly feel, came to him every night about twelve o'clock and settled upon his chest, drawing all the life out of him, so that he became paralised [*sic*] for the time being, and neither could move nor cry out. Thereupon the miller agreed to share the bed with the boy, and made him promise that he should give a certain sign when the vampire arrived. This was done, and when the signal was made the miller putting out his hands grasped an invisible but very tangible substance that rested upon the boy's chest. He described it as apparently elliptical in shape, and to the touch feeling like gelatine [*sic*], properties which suggest an ectoplasmic formation. The thing writhed and fiercely struggled to escape, but he gripped it firmly and threw it on the fire. After that the boy recovered, and there was an end of these visits.

The haglike trait of the vampire of draining away vitality and life remains its dominant characteristic in the lore of modern times. Is the vampire, then, a demon or a ghost? In folklore, it can be either. But the very closest association of the vampire is traditionally not to demons or ghosts, but to werewolves—humans cursed to shape-shift into vicious wolves at the full moon. The term *vukodlak,* as well as a host of other equivalents of *vampir,* literally means "wolf's hair." *Vampirs* were, in fact, originally thought to transform themselves into wolf form for certain periods of time, as well as into the forms of dogs, cats, donkeys, horses, and humans. Another Eastern European folklore belief holds that when werewolves die, they become vampires.

The vampire, then, is capable of a broad range of behaviors ascribed to a host of other supernatural beings and creatures. But how did the vampire come into being in the first place?

Folkloric Explanations for the Vampire

Early investigators found numerous explanations given in folklore. People who died of bloody wounds or of vampire attacks, who were criminals, arsonists, extortionists, witches, suicides, or demonically possessed were among the afflicted. So were people who died in the forest, in the mountains, or at crossroads —the latter are notorious gathering points for evil forces—and whose corpses were devoured by eagles, crows, wolves, or other wild animals. In Russia, alcoholics were believed to become vampires after death, while in parts of Eastern Europe (as well as in China), animals jumping over corpses would turn them into vampires. In Romania, bats flying over a corpse would do the same.

But this association of bats with vampires is a rare one in folklore. In fact, bats are unimportant in folklore in general except as death omens.

According to folk legend, sometimes persons doomed to become vampires at death could be identified from birth. Such defects as a split lower lip, excessive body hair, or a taillike extension of the spine, as well as a caul—an amniotic membrane— covering the head, were sure marks of fated vampirism.

Once they died and became vampires, some returned to the world of the living in order to make others suffer as the soul of the vampire suffered, and some were intent upon bedeviling living friends and family. Other vampire creatures seemed to be wanderers, drifting about in ghostly or seemingly corporeal form, especially on nights lit by a bright moon.

Early investigators such as Calmet seemed fascinated with the procedures for identifying and getting rid of suspected vampires. If a vampire was believed to be plaguing a village, the villagers would dig up a corpse and look for telltale signs. Often the identity was known—someone would claim that a specific person who had died recently was on the loose and attacking others, as in some of the examples previously given. If the identity was not known, divining procedures would be used, such as leading a white gelding ridden by an innocent boy over graves; the horse would refuse to step over the grave of the vampire.

When the corpse was exhumed, the proof of vampirism was a lack of corruption of the flesh. The appearance that hair or nails had grown, that the skin was still ruddy, or that the corpse had shifted in the coffin were taken as sure signs of the "vampire condition." The most telling sign of all was fresh blood visible on the corpse, especially exuding from the mouth and other orifices.

The vampire would be dispatched by such measures as staking the heart, cutting off the head, dismemberment and disposal in running water such as a river (as running water is a widespread folklore weapon against all evil forces), or cremation. According to numerous early reports, the vampire sometimes groaned or cried out when dispatched.

The case of Peter Plogojowitz, found in *The Vampire in Europe,* shows a typical profile of vampire behavior and identification. Plogojowitz, a farmer of Kisolova in Eastern Europe, died in 1728 at age sixty-two. Three days after his death, he appeared in his home at midnight and asked his son for food. His son complied, and the father appeared to eat it, then left. Two nights later, the father reappeared and demanded food. This time, the terrified son refused, whereupon Plogojowitz fixed him with a most threatening look. The next day, the son died. Within hours, five or six other persons in the village fell ill, suffering total exhaustion and faintness, as though they lacked blood. All said they had been visited in a dream by the dead father, who "seemed to glide into the room, catch them by the throat—biting hard—and suck the blood out of the wound." In less than a week, nine persons were dead.

Military officers then opened the grave of the elder Plogojowitz and:

> . . . found him as though he were in a trance, gently breathing, his eyes wide open and glaring horribly, his complexion ruddy, the flesh plump and full. His hair and nails had grown, and when the scarfskin came off there appeared new and healthy cuticle. His mouth was all slobbered and stained with fresh blood. Thence they at once concluded it was he who must be the Vampire thus molesting the district, and it was necessary at once to put a stop to his ravages in case he should affect the whole village. The executioner armed with a heavy mallet drove a sharp stake through his heart, during which the grave was deluged with the blood that gushed from the wound, his nose, ears, and every orifice of the body. A big pyre of logs and brushwood having been built, the body was placed thereon. It was dry weather and the wood when kindled soon burned brightly, the flames being fanned by a gentle breeze. In a very short time the body was reduced to ashes. No marks of vampirism being found upon the other bodies, they were reburied with due precautions, garlic and whitethorn being placed in the coffins, and thenceforth the village was freed from any molestations.

A shrieking vampire of record is found in the case of Arnold Paole, which took place in the same general area a year earlier, in 1727. Paole, a soldier from Medvegia (Meduegna), was stationed for a while in Greece. There he became acquainted with the local beliefs that the dead return to haunt the living, and furthermore discovered, to his horror, that his company was stationed at a particularly haunted site. One night, he had a visitation from what he believed was a vampire. The next day, Summers says, Paole "sought the unhallowed grave and executed summary vengeance upon the Vampire." He then resigned from the army and returned home. Despite his engagement to marry, Paole remained moody and depressed. He finally confessed to his fiancé that ever since he had been visited by the vampire, he had had a premonition of early death. The premonition came true. One day he fell off a hay wagon and was knocked unconscious. He languished in bed for a time and died.

About a month later, reports began to circulate that his form was seen wandering about the village after dark. Several persons stated that they were being haunted by him, and afterward always felt "a state of extraordinary debility." After a number of deaths, the villagers were gripped by panic and began remaining indoors after dusk. Still, it was said Paole could penetrate locked doors and barred windows.

Some ten weeks after Paole's burial, the villagers decided his corpse must be exhumed and examined for signs of vampirism:

It was seen that the corpse had moved to one side, and the jaws gaped wide open and the blub lips were moist with new blood which had trickled in a thin stream from the corner of the mouth. All unafraid the sexton caught the body and twisted it straight. "So," he cried, "You have not wiped your mouth since last night's work." Even the officers of the battlefield and the surgeons accustomed to the horrors of the dissecting room shuddered at so hideous a spectacle. It is recorded that the drummer boy swooned on the spot.

Nerving themselves to their awful work, they inspected the remains more closely, and it was soon apparent that there lay before them the thing they dreaded—the vampire. He looked, indeed, as if he had not been dead a day. On handling the corpse the scarfskin came off, and below there were new skin and new nails. Accordingly they scattered garlic over the remains and drove a stake through the body, which it is said gave a piercing shriek as the warm blood spouted out in a great crimson jet.

When this dreadful operation had been performed they proceeded to exhume the bodies of four others who had died in consequence of Arnold's attacks. The records give no details of the state in which these were found. They simply say that whitethorn stakes were driven through them and that they were all five burned. The ashes of all were replaced in consecrated ground.

Modern researchers have attempted to find natural explanations for the "vampire condition." Premature burial, not uncommon in days of more primitive medical knowledge, has been put forward as a cause, and may account for some cases. The most likely natural explanation is that the symptoms shown by the allegedly afflicted corpses were merely normal signs of decomposition. As Paul Barber explains in *Vampires, Burial, and Death: Folklore and Reality* (1988), the buildup of gases in a decomposing body can not only make it shift in the coffin, but can make it move and sit up as though alive. The gases can also force the corpse's own blood out from the lungs through the mouth and orifices. The "new" nails seen by vampire hunters may not have been new at all, but simply the glossy beds underneath the old nails, which slough off in decomposition. Decomposing corpses often do take on a ruddy color, which vampire hunters took as a sign of prolonged life as opposed to the ashen color of death. And finally, the alleged "piercing shriek" given by Paole could be explained by the fact that it's not unusual for corpses to emit sounds when moved or disturbed, as by a stake through the heart. The sounds are caused by a compression of the chest cavity that forces air past the glottis. Thus, it would be unusual for a staked corpse *not* to make noise that would sound like groans or moans. As for the "shriek" in the Paole case, perhaps that was a bit of embroidering for the sake of drama.

Such rational explanations may indeed account for some alleged vampires, but perhaps not all cases. Certainly, in the eighteenth century, all people had to deal with were strange and frightening accounts of something beyond belief.

Romancing the Vampire

When lurid vampire reports began reaching the Western public, they stimulated artistic imagination, and from there, the folklore vampire passed directly into the land of fantasy. Romanticized vampires began appearing in stories, poems, and novels.

The first story to fuse vampire elements into a literary genre was "The Vampyre," written in 1816 by twenty-year-old John Polidori, an Italian immigrant who was briefly employed as the Romantic poet Lord Byron's physician. Polidori wrote the story over two or three idle mornings following his dismissal by Byron. He borrowed heavily from "Fragment of a Story," part of an unpublished ghost story with vampiric details told by Byron during the famous evening of story-telling among friends that also yielded Mary Shelley's idea for *Frankenstein*. Polidori had also been present, along with the poet Percy Bysshe Shelley, Mary's future husband.

Polidori's story lay unpublished until 1819, when it appeared in a magazine under Lord Byron's name. Byron was furious and declared, "I have a personal dislike to vampires, and the little acquaintance I have with them would by no means induce me to reveal their secrets." (However, he included vampirism in his poetry, such as in "The Giaour.") In the ensuing flap, the magazine editor resigned, and Byron quickly sought publication of his own "Fragment," *sans* vampiric details.

The vampire in Polidori's story is the mysterious but suave and seductive Lord Ruthven, whom Polidori modeled upon Lord Byron himself. Ruthven has a "dead grey eye" and "deadly hue of his face" but fascinates all who meet him, especially women. He attracts the interest of a young rich man, Aubrey, and together they travel about the Continent. There Aubrey meets a young woman who tells him about "vampyres" who subsist on the blood of young women, and he realizes that Lord Ruthven has the same characteristics. The young woman is attacked by a vampire and killed, and Aubrey also is attacked. After he and Lord Ruthven resume their travels, they are beset by bandits and Lord Ruthven is mortally wounded. Ruthven makes Aubrey swear not to reveal his death back in England. He further orders the robbers to expose his corpse to the "first cold ray of the moon."

Aubrey returns to England, where he is astonished

to see Lord Ruthven show up at parties as though nothing had happened to him—yet Aubrey had seen him die in Europe. Nonetheless, he is honor-bound not to say anything. To his horror, Lord Ruthven becomes betrothed to his sister. Aubrey, near insanity, tries to prevent it, but the two are married. Aubrey is deemed insane, and the newlyweds leave London. Aubrey finally manages to send off a warning to his sister, but it arrives too late. The story ends: "The guardians hastened to protect Miss Aubrey; but when they arrived, it was too late. Lord Ruthven had disappeared, and Aubrey's sister had glutted the thirst of a VAMPYRE!"

Thus, we have the sketch of today's vampire antihero.

The image was built upon in subsequent literary efforts. Among those of note is *Varney the Vampire,* an 800-page novel by Thomas Preskett Prest published in 1847. *Varney,* a "penny-dreadful," as Gothic horror stories were called at the time, features another aristocratic, albeit uncharming, vampire: Sir Francis Varney, who preys upon the Bannerworth family. Varney is out not only for their blood but for their family home as well.

Also influential was Sheridan Le Fanu's novella *Carmilla* (1872), about a lesbian relationship between a young woman who lives in a castle in Austria and a stranger, Carmilla, who comes to stay. Carmilla is secretly a vampire, having once been the Countess Mircalla Karnstein who'd died 150 years previously. Carmilla is unmasked and destroyed.

The most famous literary vampire creation, and the one to set the standard for all fictional vampires to come, was Bram Stoker's *Dracula*. Stoker created a story from an ingenious mix of historical fact, folklore, and pure fantasy, and changed forever the image of the vampire in modern collective unconscious in the West. He named his vampire Dracula after a fifteenth-century Wallachian ruler, Prince Vlad III Tepes (1431–1476), called Dracula ("son of the devil," as *dracul* means "devil") for his numerous cruelties and atrocities against his enemies and subjects alike. Tepes was fond of torturing people in the most barbaric manner possible—he would cut off the breasts of mothers and stuff them with the severed heads of their children before executing them by impaling them on stakes. There was not a shred of association of Tepes with supernatural vampirism, yet because Stoker borrowed the name, a belief persists today that Tepes was a vampire.

Stoker mixed in generous amounts of folklore about vampires, but, like any good novelist, didn't let facts stand in the way of a good story. He made up what he needed in order to spin a good tale. For example, Stoker's vampires had to sleep in their native earth; hence, when Dracula decides to move to England, he must transport coffins lined with his native soil. This evidently was Stoker's invention, for it appears nowhere in vampire folklore.

Stoker also borrowed liberally from the folklore of werewolves, so much so that one could say that Dracula was more werewolf than vampire. "Stoker's descriptions of Count Dracula as having long pointed fingernails, pointed ears, hair on the palms of his hands, and the extended canine fangs seem taken from werewolf cases of record," said Allen J. Gittens, founder and president of the original Vampyre Society in Chippenham, England. "Dracula had immense control over wolves. He frequently summoned wolf packs. He traveled to England and left the ship *Demeter* in the form of what was described as an immense dog, but was probably a wolf. And he controlled the wolf Berserker that escaped from the London zoo and burst through Lucy Westenra's window."

In addition, it is evident that Stoker had an enormous amount of fun writing *Dracula,* for he larded it with inside jokes and plays on words for his family and circle of friends. In America, a popular theory among literary critics holds that *Dracula* is the product of the repressed sexual tension of the Victorian era. This view is eschewed in England as the unfortunate product of a sex-obsessed culture.

"[It is] absolute rubbish," declared Bernard Davies, who is arguably the world's greatest expert on Stoker's novel. Davies, cofounder and chairman of the Count Dracula Society in London, has spent some twenty years poring over every innuendo in *Dracula,* attempting to sleuth out all of Stoker's jokes. *"Dracula* is full of in jokes," Davies told me. "People don't realize this. Except me, because I've found many of them. Stoker wrote the whole thing with his tongue in his cheek. When he was doing the finished text, he interlarded it with little references, particularly for friends and relatives, that they would recognize." Such little jokes included names and plays on names, and fictionalized descriptions of real houses and places. (While there is not room here for a full literary analysis of *Dracula,* readers who desire a behind-the-scenes look at the novel can consult Leonard Wolf's magnificent book *The Annotated Dracula* (1975). It is, alas, out of print, but may be found in some libraries or through used- and rare-book dealers.)

Stoker also drew on the professional career of his close friend, actor Henry Irving—he was impressed with the way Irving's eyes always seemed to glint red, said Davies—and drew on previous literary works, including *Carmilla* and *Trilby*. The character of Svengali in *Trilby* by George du Mâurier may have served as a model for the imperious Count: Both are older men wielding influence over young women, and both dress entirely in black.

While Stoker revolutionized the popular image of the vampire, he still didn't deliver the sexual, erotic, romantic figure we have in pop culture today. While the Count's preying upon young women may be seen as having sexual overtones, the figure of the Count himself was anything but erotic. According to Stoker's description, he was tall, old, clean-shaven except for a long white mustache, clad head to foot in black, and had bushy eyebrows that met over his nose, breath that smelled like a charnel house, lice-infested hair, pointed ears, a thin nose, sharp teeth, hairy palms, and long and sharp pointed nails. Hardly a Don Juan.

The job of romanticizing Dracula was left to Hamilton Dean, the son of a friend of Stoker's. Dean adapted *Dracula* for the stage. In his interpretation, Dracula was presented as a suave, sophisticated gentleman in evening dress. The movie *Dracula* was adapted more from the stage play than from the novel, and when the magnetic Bela Lugosi appeared as the sophisticated Count, women the world over swooned for him and letters with marriage proposals poured in by the thousands.

By today's standards, Lugosi seems stiff and almost comic, but at the time, women found his exotic nature, commanding presence, accent, and steely gaze irresistible. The erotic vampire was born, becoming progressively sexier and more seductive through the performances of charismatic actors such as Christopher Lee, Louis Jourdan, and Frank Langella.

The only films of note to portray Dracula as Stoker envisioned him were the two versions of *Nosferatu*. The original 1922 film, by F. W. Murnau and starring Max Schreck as Count Orlock, was a plagiarism of Stoker's novel, which Stoker's widow, Florence, succeeded in having pulled from the market. All copies were ordered destroyed, but one survived. An authorized version of the film was made in 1979 starring Klaus Kinski. *Nosferatu,* which means "undead," features an ugly, ratlike vampire with long, pointed nails and two front teeth that are long and sharp and better suited for biting than canine teeth. In Romanian folklore, *nosferatu* refers to the Devil, and is a reanimated corpse that sucks the blood of others. Romanian folklore refers to vampires as *strigoi,* also reanimated corpses, which can assume the shapes of various evil animals—though not the bat.

In literature also, the vampire has been liberated from his ugliness. One immediately thinks of the sensual creatures who populate Anne Rice's vampire novels, but the real credit goes to author Chelsea Quinn Yarbro according to Margaret L. Carter, an expert on vampires in literature. Yarbro has penned a number of vampire novels, the best-known of which is

Hotel Transylvania (1978), featuring the legendary Comte de Saint Germain as a wealthy, sophisticated, glamorous, and immortal vampire who moves with ease in the world of the living.

"Certainly Anne Rice has had a lot of influence, but in terms of revolutionizing the vampire, I attribute that to Yarbro," Carter said. "Her vampires are much more straightforwardly sympathetic, altogether nice people, much nicer than the human beings around them. Her vampires are noble . . . in a human world where things are so brutal the vampires would look kind anyway."

The best-known modern vampires are those in Anne Rice's books *Interview with the Vampire* (1976), *The Vampire Lestat* (1984), and *The Queen of the Damned* (1988). Rice's immortal vampires are beautiful creatures graced with supernormal powers of strength, speed, and heightened senses, and they live in a world of wealth, sophistication, and splendor. Their blood-drinking is for most of them a sensual, erotic exercise, substituting for their inability to perform sexually as mortals do. Some are moralists, worried about their inherent evil. Rice's vampires are about as far from folklore vampirism as one can get.

In *Interview with the Vampire,* Rice provides an opportunity for her beautiful vampires to meet the vampires of Slavic folklore. Louis, the protagonist and narrator of the book, and the child vampire Claudia travel to the Old World in a quest to find their own roots and answer their questions about their existence. What they find is a handful of mindless monsters roaming about in rotting clothing, stinking of the grave. The villagers fear these monsters, ward them off with the traditional garlic, and stake them through the heart when they discover them.

But when it comes to explaining how these traditional vampires are so different from the sophisticated likes of Louis and Claudia, Rice skirts the issue. Louis only comments, "I had my theories. So did Claudia." Claudia opines that the deranged behavior is due to vampire victims, now vampires themselves in death, going mad from blood lust while struggling to escape their coffins.

What is accurate about Rice's depiction is that there was nothing glamorous about old-world vampires.

"Ethnic vampirism was much more gross, much more down-market, much more repulsive," observed Bernard Davies. "Frankly, there's nothing very erotic about vampirism. Being gnashed in the neck by your lately dead mother-in-law—who was probably a bit of a dog, as you Americans would say—there's nothing particularly sexy about that, is there? These were the types of people who vampirized you in ethnic vampirism. This bit about the elegant count or countess with a ring on every finger and beautifully dressed, sweeping through the village, having *droit du seigneur* with all the peasants is a load of rubbish. To start with, vampirism was chiefly familial—you vampirized your relatives, not strangers. You can imagine the condition of some of the peasants after they'd led a toilsome peasant life for some sixty or seventy years. No, there's nothing very romantic about it *at all*. This to me is total disconnection from what really happened. Forget the literary business. What you got in ethnic vampirism was filthy, disgusting old peasant men and women, and who wants to be leched up in the night by old Uncle Boris who's got no teeth anyway?"

Davies is right, but it's a point that falls on deaf ears out there in Medialand. The sexy, glamorous vampire—a creature who is 99 percent fantasy—has become a permanent pop icon.

Chapter Four

An Endless Fascination

IT IS INCREASINGLY APPARENT THAT THE EXISTENCE OF vampires operates largely as a matter of belief. In fact, *belief* is the key word in Vampire Reality.

In the previous chapter, we explored several reported cases of "real vampires" in Eastern Europe. Collective belief in the vampire was strong, even though the vampire took various forms. When certain experiences happened, they were explained in terms of the vampire—and then the villagers went looking for the physical evidence, in the form of an uncorrupted corpse, to corroborate the experiences. Outsiders, who did not share the same reality, looked for other explanations. However, their disbelief did not negate the reality of the Eastern Europeans' experiences.

We also saw in the previous chapter how the image of the vampire changed to suit a different collective point of view. The Slavic vampire came to the attention of Western culture at a time when society had a collective romance with death, and later a fear and denial of it. The vampire lost its repulsive, ghostly nature and became an immortal physical being. It evolved from eternally damned villain to glamorous antihero, one with certain graces and certain weaknesses shaped by holdovers from folklore, and one with an inner life of its own. "We can empathize with vampires no matter how evil they are if we can get inside their minds," observed Margaret L. Carter concerning the literary vampire.

In literature, the vampire has provided a means for examining perennial questions about existence and the nature of evil. The vampire is admired for his denial of death and his ability to transcend the dullness of mundane human life. How glamorous life would be, it seems, if we, too, lived forever, suffered no illness, had no wants, and were able to rise above the plodding human masses.

Yet the vampire is profoundly alienated from all other living things, as we in modern times feel alienated from our own societies. Thus, we identify with the vampire's pain. The evil of his subsistence on blood—his taking of life in order to sustain his own—is a reflection of humanity's collective struggle to come to terms with its own inherent evil.

Mostly, however, today's audience finds the vampire glamorous. The vampire is unique, exotic, alluring, romantic, sexy, appealing, sophisticated. A breed apart. Distinguished. Thus, it is no surprise that, in a desire to rise above our ordinariness, our humdrum lives, some of us look to the vampire as either an escape or an ideal. If the desire is strong enough, the vampire becomes a real presence.

How do people express their interest in vampires?

How do vampires manifest to the believers? For answers, we can turn to some of the individuals and organizations that study and serve the vampire aficionado community. They hear frequently from individuals who have all manner of questions and confessions.

Letters and Phone Calls: Vampiredom's Confessionals

All vampire organizations and researchers receive more than their share of unusual mail. Those who dip into Vampire Reality, whether occasionally for entertainment or on a more serious level of involvement, seem to be dedicated letter-writers. Letters are an easy medium for catharsis and expression, and vampires and vampire enthusiasts seem to embrace it with a passion. They frankly record their intimate fantasies, longings, and experiences. Some letter-writers sign their real names, some do not. Some give addresses for replies and conduct an ongoing correspondence that is deeply personal, yet curiously impersonal because there is never any face-to-face contact. Many more letter-writers are never heard from again, nor do they respond to replies. They rise out of oblivion, flame into momentary brightness, and, having released themselves, sink back into that same oblivion.

Along with letters come unusual phone calls. Like letter-writers, callers seem to want to get something off their chests or relieve anxieties. Again, some may identify themselves while others do not.

Jeanne K. Youngson, president and founder of the Count Dracula Fan Club in New York City, has been on the front lines of Vampire Reality since she founded the organization more than twenty-five years ago. She talked about some of her experiences during the numerous meetings we had at the Manhattan quarters of the club's museum. The club boasts perhaps the world's largest collection of vampire books and objects—everything imaginable has been turned into a vampire or makes use of the vampire image— most collected over the years by Youngson. They are crammed onto shelves and into display cases. For example, did you know that some clever manufacturer made ice buckets shaped like coffins, with little Count Draculas inside? There are Dracula candles, puppets, light fixtures, wind socks, games, puzzles, candy, Christmas ornaments (no need to consign vampires merely to Halloween), windup dolls, key chains, soaps, ad infinitum.

Youngson became interested in vampires in 1965, following a visit to Romania during which she learned about Vlad Tepes serving as a role model for Stoker's fictional Count Dracula. Stoker's novel had long fascinated Youngson, and she got the idea of forming a fan club. The club publishes two newsletters and an assortment of small books and pamphlets.

Youngson said she never knows what she is going to find in a letter or at the other end of the telephone.

"Calls seem to come in bunches," she said. "One week I might hear from two or three people, and then not from anybody for a while. Some people I've been talking to off and on since 1978. Sometimes I feel like a counselor. I say to some of them, 'Tell me about yourself.' That's all you have to say to people—they love to talk about themselves and what their interests are. I very seldom have to ask more than one or two questions. Unfortunately, some just call or write once or twice and then disappear, and leave me wondering what's happened. There are a lot of unfinished novels out there."

"How would you characterize the kinds of calls and letters you get?" I asked Youngson.

"We have several categories of people," she answered. "Some have no interest in joining the club, but think they're vampires or have been told they're vampires and they want to get it off their chests, somebody sympathetic to talk to. It must be like going to a confessional, except a lot of them don't dare do that out of fear of what the priests will say. What they want is somebody to talk to who is not going to tell them they're rotten because they want to drink someone's blood. A lot of them seem upset. Others have accepted this about themselves.

"Very often I can tell from the first few words the direction they're going to go. If they say they want to unload, they want me to say, 'You're not as sick as people are telling you or you think you are.' There are others whom I have referred to a psychiatrist if they are suffering from great anxiety."

Some of Youngson's letter-writers and callers are obviously out for laughs. Others are engaged in a painful self-exploration. "Some are very bright, and it helps to get the words out so that they can clarify what's going on in their lives by hearing themselves talk," Youngson said. "I've often thought—and I've never told anybody this—that if they sat down and wrote out their whole scenario, they could find the secret of whatever it is they're looking for."

Occasionally people call or write looking for partners for sadomasochistic sex. Youngson quickly and firmly turns them away and discourages further communication.

Many calls and letters are filled with trivia on what life is like as a self-professed vampire. "You find out what vampires look like and dress like," Youngson said. "They stay up at night and stay inside with the curtains drawn during the daytime. I never wanted to be a vampire because I love the sun too much. Some people say they have a physical need for blood. But I think sometimes people just try to psych themselves into thinking this. One of the first persons I ever talked to was a kid whose parents both worked and he had a lot of time to himself. He became a pseudovampire. At night he would go hang out in a cemetery and lie on top of tombstones. He was also into some weird sexual practices like self-fellatio."

Youngson said vampire fantasies also had alleviated the boredom of a housewife from Lodi, California. "She wrote and told me her story. Her children were grown and her husband was a long-distance trucker. So, she decided to become a vampire because she was bored. When she was growing up, she had an uncle and was always crazy about him. He died and became her male vampire figure. She writes herself sexy love letters and pushes them under the door so that she'll find them when she comes back from shopping."

Youngson noted that while fantasies vary, the blood-drinkers who contact her almost universally share one real-life circumstance. "Almost everyone I have talked to, with very few exceptions, has had a very unhappy childhood. Rejection, being abused.

Quite a few can identify where they get their craving for blood from—they can pinpoint the exact circumstances. Sometimes there is a definite pivotal point, such as an accident or an incident of sexual abuse."

I asked Youngson what person had made the most impact on her. She thought for a moment. "The most unusual was a lesbian named M—— L—— whom I met in 1981. She called and asked if she could meet with me. Although M.L. looked tough and sounded tough, she was a sensitive person. She was kind of stocky with short hair and was dressed in a white T-shirt and jeans. She had a pack of cigarettes rolled up in one sleeve. All up and down her arms were the scars of slashes and cuts where she had sliced herself with a razor so that her girlfriend could drink her blood. They also exchanged menstrual blood, which didn't bother her but did bother her girlfriend. She said she worked in a nightclub on the East Side. Her story was that the girlfriend came to the club with her husband one night. The girl was not a lesbian, but the husband treated his wife badly. She went back to the club alone and M.L. was nice to her. They ended up going to San Francisco together.

"M.L.'s pivotal point apparently was sexual abuse in childhood by an uncle. When she was ten and eleven, he made her go down on him. She seemed to mimic him in some ways. She mentioned that he used to keep his cigarettes rolled up in his sleeve and she did the same thing.

"It was the first and only time I ever talked to someone who had attended a Black Mass on the Upper East Side," Youngson said. "They slit the throat of a dog and drank the blood. I don't like to hear things like that, but it's part of my job. I can't stand b-l-o-o-d anyway, but as long as I don't see it, I'm okay."

Youngson's "favorite vampire" is Rose [a pseudonym], who actually is a recovered blood fetishist. Rose is Youngson's favorite because she is shy and has a sweet and gentle nature. Rose started thinking of herself as a vampire in her teen years, when she experienced intense cravings for blood. Even before then, as a child, she was obsessed with blood and equated it with love. For much of her early adult life, Rose consumed small amounts of human blood, sharing with a donor or finding unusual ways to acquire it. Now in her fifties, she lives a reclusive life on the East Coast. She has been diagnosed as schizophrenic and is an outpatient at a mental health facility. She has no job and lives with her mother on a small support income. She agreed to tell me her story through a series of letters.

Rose traces her troubles, including her obsession with blood, to the severe abuse she suffered in childhood. Her early life was unsettled and unhappy and she felt unwanted by her parents, who fought constantly. When she was seven, her father abandoned the family. Her mother was incapable of caring for her, and she was sent to a Catholic boarding school. There the lesson about Christ shedding his blood out of love for humanity was drummed into her by the nuns. The images of the bleeding hearts of Jesus, Mary, and a host of blessed martyrs made a powerful impact upon her—poor unworthy sinner that she felt herself to be.

"I was about ten when I became obsessed by the idea of Christ's blood being shed for us," Rose said.

"Of course, I'd received religious training long before that, but it took a couple of years before the images and ideas sank into my subconscious mind. Christ's blood represented *love*, as he loved us so much that he died for us."

When her mother's money ran out as Rose neared adolescence, Rose was removed from boarding school and given over to her grandparents. Under their care, she suffered beatings and other abuse. From the ages of twelve to fifteen, her life was a nightmare. For escape, Rose turned to horror and science fiction comic books that she read in secret. During this period, she learned that her mother's ancestors came from Romania, and this knowledge fueled her growing obsession with blood. The symbolism of blood as love became entwined with that of blood as power, for fantasy told her that the vampires of Eastern Europe drank blood and enjoyed supernatural powers. Rose would daydream about being a powerful vampire or a werewolf.

"I first got the urge to drink blood at age twelve, when my periods started," Rose said. "I used to stick myself with pins and rose thorns and lick the blood. I basically drank my own blood, and I repressed my urge to 'snack' on other people. I felt guilty about my abnormal desire, but I fed my urge by reading vampire stories and going to see vampire movies. I definitely kept my thoughts a deep *secret*. I considered myself a vampire because I was obsessed with the occult and the idea of drinking *blood*."

Rose lived this life as a secret vampire until she graduated from college and entered the teaching profession. Then her blood-drinking took a new turn. "I first drank the blood of others at age twenty-one, when

I was a teacher," she said. "The tots used to fall down and get hurt at recess. I blotted their scrapes with cotton swabs, and I saved the cotton to 'snack' on later. I never got blood any other way, and I *never* bit anyone." She continued to keep her habit secret.

Rose worked as a teacher from 1961 to 1972. She quit out of a growing frustration and disillusionment with the increasing disaffection of the students. For several years she was out of work, and then in 1975 landed a job as a saleslady in a women's clothing shop. The job lasted until 1980, when the shop went out of business.

Most of her co-workers were of an ethnic group that put great faith in magical spells as remedies for life's problems. Rose, who by this time was well read in the occult arts, offered to perform spells for them in exchange for blood. The client would prick a finger and drip several drops of blood onto a clean piece of paper. Rose would take the paper home, lick the blood from it and then perform the desired spell with colored candles. "My candle spells were taken partly from books on magic and partly from my own inspiration," she said. She estimated that about 80 percent of the spells were successful. "They depended on *faith*, and, as you know, faith can move mountains."

Around 1979, two life-changing events took place for Rose. Her schizophrenia was diagnosed. It was brought on, she said, by her worry over her mother's old age and chronic ill health. And she met a blood fetishist, an older woman who became her donor for blood-drinking. Tanya [a pseudonym] was introduced to Rose through Martin V. Riccardo (see more on him later in this chapter). It seemed to Rose that at last she had found a kindred soul.

Tanya lived in New York City, and Rose was able to visit her there four or five times a year. In the privacy of Tanya's apartment, they would prick each other's fingers with sterilized needles and lancets and suck blood. Rose found it a somewhat painful process but didn't mind the pain. "Blood-drinking made me feel special," Rose said. "But I also felt rather ashamed and guilty. I had a confused self-image." Her desire for blood, however, was stronger than her shame and guilt.

Tanya told Rose she was not really a vampire, but a blood fetishist. She explained the difference between vampires, beings with supernatural powers, and blood fetishists, humans who have cravings for blood. Rose changed her self-image and began calling herself a blood fetishist.

Tanya was involved with vampire research and fan organizations on both sides of the Atlantic. She drew Rose into these circles and engaged her in various activities. Rose met Youngson and struck up a friendship that they maintain to the present. Tanya also brought Rose into a correspondence with Sean Manchester in England (see Chapter Five), and introduced her to an author of numerous occult books and horror novels.

At the time, the author was researching material for a book on vampires. He asked Rose to suck his blood. "He wanted to find out what it was like," Rose said. "He expected it to be an exotic experience." She went to the man's Manhattan apartment on the afternoon of June 17, 1980. The encounter was a disaster. "Unfortunately, it was terribly painful for him," she said. "He kept yelping in pain that I was hurting him. And I was terribly upset, because I did *not* want to cause him pain! He discovered that having his blood taken was *not* the thrilling and exciting experience he'd imagined it to be. I was *unnerved* because he treated me as if I was some kind of crazed fiend! We never saw each other again."

Rose then decided to confess something else that had occurred that afternoon, and which also had a devastating effect on her. "He seduced me!" she said. "I was a very naive, starry-eyed virgin with *no* experience, and I believed him when he told me that I looked just like his late wife. He also told me that he wanted a 'long-term' relationship. Well, long-term for him was a one-night stand! It was such a *disaster* that I never had sex again! I am totally celibate!"

Over time Rose discovered that Tanya had political and sexual interests, that, Rose said, "turned me *off* completely! She dominated me, while I complained about my subservient position." Rose terminated the relationship with Tanya in 1981. Although the author wrote that the two women had shared their blood while lying together in long embraces, Rose denies that such ever took place. "You can't take blood or give it while both partners are prone," she said. She explained that the easiest way to exchange blood is for the donor to sit while the taker stands. She said that Tanya and the author were her only blood donors.

Rose began treatment for her schizophrenia, the chief symptoms of which were hearing imaginary voices and suffering a pervading sense of panic. She was able to give up blood-drinking. "I don't 'snack' on folks now," she said. "As one psychiatrist said to me, 'It is socially inappropriate.' So is picking your nose! Although counseling helped, the *real* factor in giving up blood-drinking was the fear of the incurable disease AIDS. I stopped 'snacking' in 1982. I don't miss it as much as I thought I would. I sublimate with vampire novels and films.

"Very few people know about my blood-drinking, except for a handful of vampire researchers and the people at the mental health center. Folks at the mental health center overlook my former 'snacking' habits and accept me for myself. I've made some friends among the other clients at the center. We have parties and planned outings for the 'mental health consumers,' which is what mental patients are called these days. I really enjoy the group outings. I feel that I am fairly well adjusted since I stopped drinking blood."

Across the East River from the Count Dracula Fan Club in Brooklyn is the Vampire Information Exchange (VIE), run by Eric S. Held, a public-school teacher. Held became interested in vampires in 1972 through an artist friend who drew vampires, and who introduced him to Stoker's *Dracula*. One night Held heard a radio talk show featuring Stephen Kaplan, founder and president of the Vampire Research Center. He contacted Kaplan later and was referred to a woman named Dorothy Nixon who lived in upstate New York. Nixon and Held began a phone friendship that led to the formation of the VIE with themselves as the initial and only members. Membership has increased steadily ever since. The organization caters to fans of vampire fiction and film, and those who want to learn more about the vampire in folklore.

Nixon dropped out several years ago, and Held now runs the VIE himself. He publishes a small newsletter that includes names and addresses of members who so desire; many are looking for like-minded pen pals. Stimulating correspondence is one of two purposes of the VIE; the other is the dissemination of information about vampires in fact and fiction.

Held has a formidable collection of vampire books, films on videotape, and news clippings, which he shared with me one frosty winter afternoon. His interest, like Youngson's, runs to fictional vampires. Some self-professed vampires join the VIE, but Held does no matchmaking. His own opinion of vampires, he told me, is skeptical. "I don't believe there are real vampires in the classic sense," he said. "But I can picture people who *believe* they are." That's all right with him, as long as they do not try to use the VIE for unsavory pursuits such as sadomasochism and violence.

Like Youngson, Held receives strange correspondence. (He conducts business strictly by mail and not by phone.) "I get quite a few letters from people who are looking for someone to suck their blood or vice versa, and from people looking for vampire orgies. I've had people say they drink animal blood or human blood. It's weird and strange, and the handwriting in many letters is even stranger—very tilted, close together, and difficult to comprehend. Some are looking for books about casting magical spells on others, how to become a vampire, or how to prosper using their vampirism. Some say they already *are* vampires but want to become better. You never know. It's scary stuff sometimes. I usually don't say much to people who want to become vampires or become better vampires. If the letter seems harmless, I'll send information on the VIE." Held once had problems with individuals who, he discovered, were interested primarily in finding people to join an S-and-M group. He now carefully screens applicants and their answers to members' questionnaires, which he publishes in the newsletter.

"How do self-professed vampires say they became vampires?" I asked.

"One person told me that ever since she was very young, she had this feeling for blood but did not know how to use it until she became older. She will find relationships with people who will give and take blood. Another one said he was born a vampire—he was the son of a vampire. Others say they don't know how they became vampires, but they just are. I approach a lot of this tongue-in-cheek. I try to avoid controversy, I don't put anyone down. I try to be as neutral as possible.

"The scarier letters are from practicing vampires who want their identities to be kept confidential because they are afraid people are after them," Held said. "One of the scariest envelopes I got was from a woman who put razor blades around the envelope and spray-painted it in red, so that the entire envelope was red except for the outline of the blades. I don't feel personally afraid since I use a post office box, but I thought, This person is wandering around somewhere. And that scared me. To take the time to do this, and she doesn't know me at all. I ignored the envelope and sent her the information on the VIE. She joined us and stayed for about two years. She introduced herself as Countess Misty, and that's the only name I knew her by. Even the mailings to her were by that name, but that isn't unusual—I have a few people who use only aliases. Most of her writing was secretive. She would write about what she was doing and ask me not to print it. A lot of them, though, *want* to be public and are looking for people with similar interests. I don't feel like a 'Dear Abby,' but I do feel good when people get together."

Every now and then, Held receives a letter from someone who seems truly troubled and asks for help. "I had one that I wasn't sure how to handle, from a girl who told me she'd been abused as a child since an early age and asked me for help and advice," he said. "I wrote back with suggestions, from talking to friends to joining a group. A couple of months later, I received a letter back saying, 'Thank you, I'm beginning to get my own life together and you helped very much.' That's one of the nicest things that has happened."

Farther east on Long Island, in Elmhurst, New York, is the Vampire Research Center, run by Stephan Kaplan, a public-school educator. Kaplan, a self-described "brilliant promoter," founded the center in 1972 under the original name Vampire Research Center of America. The title was later shortened. The activities of collecting information on alleged vampires have been conducted by Kaplan and his wife, Roxanne Salch Kaplan, with the assistance of a staff of eight, although he said he is assisted by experts—such as endodontists and hematologists—in the course of research.

Kaplan periodically conducts a "vampire census" and releases the results to the media. He speaks of the "dangers" of being a vampirologist, and his self-promotion in the media has earned him numerous detractors.

Kaplan said he gets numerous letters and phone calls—the calls coming at all hours of the night—from people who fall into six categories: 1) those who think they have seen vampires; 2) those who claim to have been attacked by vampires; 3) those who are suspected of being vampires; 4) those who claim to be vampires; 5) those who suffer from various physical disorders; and 6) those who are interested in vampires. The center devotes itself to studying physical vampires, psychic vampires, psychological vampires, vampirelike persons ("vampiroids," as Kaplan calls them), vampire worshipers, sadomasochists, blood cults, vampire tendencies, vampire-interested people ("VIPs"), and a catchall category, "unsure and unknown types."

Kaplan defines a vampire as "an individual who must drink human blood, not as a psychological manifestation, but as a physical need." Disorders such as pernicious anemia or porphyria do not qualify, he said. This definition is rather broad—many people could say they physically "need" blood. And how does one distinguish an apparent physical need that has its origins in the psyche?

Kaplan said he believes that most persons who call the center claiming to be vampires aren't the genuine article, anyway. They are merely vampiroids, people who act like vampires. He said he has collected about 2,000 vampiroid cases over the years.

Kaplan estimates that there are some 600 "real vampires" around the world, with about 300 of them in the United States (most of those live in California).

These estimates, however, are extrapolated from meager and questionable data. Kaplan has sent out three census forms, in 1980–81, 1982–83, and 1988–89. The forms go to individuals who have contacted the center. Results are tabulated from the responses sent back. The three surveys have drawn only twenty-one, thirty-five, and twenty-five responses, respectively.

In addition, it is virtually impossible to validate the claims made by respondents. So, we must judge these figures as anecdotal material, and not scientific fact.

Out in the suburbs of Chicago, Martin V. Riccardo, a professional hypnotist and the founder and director of Vampire Studies (formerly the Vampire Studies Society), offers a clearinghouse of information about vampires. Riccardo became interested in vampires in the early 1970s after seeing Christopher Lee as Count Dracula, and hearing Leonard Wolf lecture on the vampire image. Riccardo's curiosity was also piqued by the obvious enjoyment he witnessed in others as cinema vampires bent over their victims to bite. In 1977, he launched the *Journal of Vampirism*, which he folded after about eight issues in order to make time for other vampire-related pursuits. Riccardo said he has always been interested most in the paranormal aspects of the vampire as they have been recorded in folklore—the possible out-of-body projection we saw in the previous chapter. But most people who contact him are interested in a more fleshly vampire.

"People have gone vampire crazy," he told me during a break between clients one afternoon. "Bela Lugosi would get hundreds of letters from female fans proposing marriage or wanting to get to know him. He was not picked for the role because he was a handsome man—he was picked because he was an ugly man with a foreign accent. The sensuality of the vampire made him appealing.

"What is happening lately is a tremendous repression of sexuality on a social level. The media are increasing the amount of portrayals of sexuality—in the soap operas, movies, and novels they have people jumping in and out of bed constantly—but at the same time there is a tremendous fear and apprehension about sexuality because of the diseases involved. On another level, there's a constant barrage of movies about date rapists, wife beaters, serial killers, and murderers in dating services. We have a portion of the population, especially those who are single, who are afraid to encounter new people, even though there is this constant erotic stimulation in the media. The vampire image is a fantasy outlet for some people to project a kind of forbidden sensual intimacy they're longing for but don't have in their lives. I've talked with other therapists who confirm this is a trend, a fear of intimacy in modern society.

"It's interesting that in some vampire novels, such as those by Anne Rice, it appears that the vampires are impotent," Riccardo went on. "They offer romance and intimacy without sexuality. It's this forbidden intimacy, a dark pleasure fantasy outlet, that attracts people."

Riccardo's mailbag yields the gamut of vampire fantasies, desires, and fears. "I get letters from people who have a desire to drink blood but have guilt feelings about it," he said. "Blood fetishism as a part of sexual practices is more common than most people realize. People get sexually excited by the sight of blood or by drinking blood, but they are not turned on by the image of the vampire per se. I tell blood-drinkers they should go for counseling. What I run across even more is letters from young women asking to meet real vampires. Many want the experience of being bitten and having their blood drunk. I say no, I can't help them."

One of Riccardo's stranger pieces of mail came from a woman of Romanian ancestry who had dreams of flying out at night. "She believed there was some family history of vampirism or witchcraft and claimed that there were strange marks on her arm as if she had been drained at one time," he said.

Riccardo receives many letters from young people caught up in the romance of being a vampire. It seems to make them feel special or superior, and perhaps may be a way of coping with feelings of alienation ("Okay, I'm a vampire, that's why no one understands me"). Some young people reveal they are dabbling in other areas of the occult, or in blood-drinking practices or rituals. They often have vague ideas about what it means to be a vampire, and are heavily influenced by popular film and fiction.

One such "vampire" was a girl from the southern United States who wrote to Riccardo after reading *Vampires* (1981) by Bernhardt J. Hurwood. In the book, Hurwood stated that vampires preferred to be called "sangroids," but in fact, he made up the term himself. The girl wrote that she and her friends were sangroids and were allergic to the sun—they sneezed every time they went out in daylight. She and several of the friends were satanists, too, and had been introduced to blood drinking in animal sacrifice rites. Through experimentation on each other, the youths discovered they enjoyed biting each other and cutting each other with razor blades in order to drink blood. These practices were part of sex, the writer informed Riccardo. The blood, she said, imparted a high. This blood-drinking in turn caused some of the group to become vampires, she said—they became hungry if they did not regularly drink blood, and their wounds would heal quickly.

I also encountered youths like this who would band together in groups that are like exclusive clubs. Membership in these groups usually requires a certain peculiarity and is by invitation and initiation only. The members take on vampire names, dress in punk or Gothic garb, and frequent nightclubs that cater to a similar crowd. They enjoy going out in public together in their vampire finery, reveling in the stares and attention they get from others. One such group in the Northwest consisted of teenage runaways who lived in an abandoned downtown building, and who supported themselves by panhandling and thievery. Their clothing of choice was not punk, however, but retro-Victorian.

Blood-drinking in vampire youth groups usually consists of draining the watery blood from packaged meat bought at the grocery, or of lapping at pricks and cuts made on each other with needles, razors, and knives.

Some of these vampire groups offer involved secret lives to members. They have their own histories, rites, and truths concerning vampires, and hierarchies of vampires. It is possible for a member to become completely caught up in the lore and the lifestyle, to the point where one "becomes" a vampire. They live fully in Vampire Reality, feeling they have undergone a physical change that includes a slowing of the aging process, immunity to illness and disease, and heightened senses and strength.

These self-made vampire groups typically are short-lived, however, breaking apart when key members, or enough members, must move on with their lives in the workaday world.

Members of one such pack that was active in the Southwestern United States said that they were either half-vampire or full vampire, transformations that required bites by persons who were half or full vampire. They said real vampires resembled Anne Rice's fictional vampires, and had supernormal senses and physical strength, were sensitive to sunlight and were resistant to disease and illness. Their immortality consisted of a series of lives in which they reincarnated into bodies with the same appearance, so that it would appear to mortals that they lived forever. The sight of blood caused them to "vamp out," or become agitated and perhaps even violent in a desire to drink blood. They obtained their blood from rare or uncooked meat, human donors, and occasionally unwilling "victims." Pack members dressed in black and were part of the punk and progressive music scene, a prerequisite, they said, for becoming a vampire. None was involved in Satanism; in fact, they abhorred satanic practices and cults. One of their favorite pack outings was to see movies like Clive Barker's horror film, *Night Breed*.

* * *

Pushing west to San Francisco, I found John L. Vellutini, the creator of the esteemed *Journal of Vampirology*. The journal was Vellutini's sole involvement in the subject of vampires; he has no organization, but he often hears from the same types of people as do the others in the field. Vellutini has published the journal on an irregular basis from 1984 to 1990, when he was forced to fold it for personal reasons. It was his practice to spend months in meticulous research for articles, all of which carried copious citations and footnotes. He examined his subjects from a variety of perspectives, including anthropology, criminology, folklore, medicine, mythology, and psychopathology.

His own interests lean toward the ethnology of the vampire—the vampire in non-Western cultures—as well as to hemocide, or murder committed in order to assuage a craving for blood, and the medical aspects of vampirism, i.e., its relation to such conditions as pernicious anemia, porphyria, rabies, and allergies. He is also open to the offbeat: He once interpreted Stoker's *Dracula* within the context of the Revelation of St. John, and also entertained the possibility of an extraterrestrial origin of vampires.

Vellutini became interested in vampires in the early 1970s while attending San Francisco State University. There, he attended a class taught by Leonard Wolf on the vampire in literature. During his research on his term paper for the class, Vellutini visited a used bookstore that had recently purchased the library of a deceased mortician. "Intrigued by what a mortician might read, I rummaged through his earthly effects and came across a dog-eared book titled *The Princi-*

ples and Practices of Embalming," he said. "Mesmerized by the ghoulish contents of the book, I decided, serendipitously as it turned out, to purchase it. Upon reading the book, I realized how public ignorance concerning the metabolic processes governing physical death may have greatly contributed to the belief in vampires in the past. The book made me realize how a likewise ignorance of the nature and transmission of disease may have been a major contributing factor as well." Vellutini continued his research on vampirism and began amassing a library of information.

He told me he takes a rationalist approach to vampires. "Ironically, I do not believe in the reality of vampirism, at least not in its traditional sense," he said. "Although I do not gainsay the possibility of discarnate spirits as psychic leeches, I believe most aspects of the vampire legend can be explained within purely rational terms. I personally maintain that the belief in vampires is derived largely from three sources: the universal fear of the dead and its concomitant psychological impact, ignorance concerning those biological processes ensuing after death, and likewise ignorance of the nature and transmission of disease."

I asked Vellutini if he had ever encountered individuals who claimed to be vampires. He said that he had interviewed, either in person or by mail, five or six self-professed vampires, but had found it a "most distasteful task."

"In every instance I sensed their vampirism was simply incidental to their perverse sexual appetites or a ceremonial adjunct to their belief in satanism," he said. "I have not remained in contact with my informants, some of whom were engaged in activities that were clearly illegal. Quite frankly, I find most latter-day 'vampires' affectatious in their manner and a far cry from their traditional counterparts. I refer to these individuals in my writings as 'hemophilists,' since the only thing they have in common with the legendary vampire is the need for blood. I say 'need' rather than 'craving,' as the requisite blood once obtained is not always consumed. Sometimes it is used as a sexual stimulant and sometimes applied toward some ritualistic purpose.

"Admittedly, there are some individuals—thankfully, in the minority—who develop an addiction to blood. This blood fetish, in my estimation, is the result of some deeply rooted mental disturbance, and individuals so afflicted are in greater need of psychological assistance than of some silly vampirologist encouraging their potentially dangerous delusions. I know some psychiatrists claim that vampirism is a distinct clinical entity in its own right, but I strongly disagree with this position. The craving for blood is but a sign or symptom of something more profound, and I have found that many self-professed 'vampires' were physically abused or shamefully neglected as children."

While vampire mania might seem to be a typically American phenomenon—Americans throw themselves so wholeheartedly into their passions—I found a keen interest in the subject across the Atlantic. After all, Ireland gave us Stoker and Le Fanu, England gave us Byron and Polidori (by way of immigration), and the Victorian era set by Queen Victoria herself gave us the artistic glorification of death.

The Vampyre Society, based in Chippenham, England, was founded by Allen J. Gittens as a result of an article on vampires he published in a music fan magazine in 1987. Prior to that, Gittens, interested in vampires for as long as he can remember, had participated in the Vampire Information Exchange (VIE) and Count Dracula Fan Club (CDFC). He began corresponding with people in England who saw his article. One of those persons was Carole Bohanon, who suggested she be a partner when Gittens formalized his organization. He agreed. The partnership worked for about a year and then split on an unhappy note. Bohanon formed her own Vampyre Society, claiming the right to use the name. At the time of my interview with Gittens, the matter was still unresolved, and Bohanon declined to speak to me. Gittens had rebuilt his organization and was pursuing his own course.

The day I ventured out from London by train to Chippenham, nestled in the Wiltshire countryside near Bath, seemed like a prime candidate for the hottest and most humid day of the year. The heat was positively wilting; yet when I alighted at the Chippenham station, Gittens, all decked out in Gothic black, somehow managed to look cool as a cucumber. Once we became engrossed in the subject of vampires, the heat was forgotten. We spent a comfortable day amidst his books and tapes, then adjourned to a local pub for a late lunch.

I asked him if he believed in vampires.

"That's a very knotty question," he replied. "I

would like to believe that there is something beyond the purely physical. Everybody has got a need deep inside them to believe in something that they can put their faith in and don't have to have proof of. I would love to have that belief in vampires, but so far I've fallen short of it. I think I understand what constitutes a vampire. I have researched vampirism from a legendary point of view and an occult point of view, and I've read very extensively about magic. I've tried to understand how such a thing as a vampire could be. On the other hand, I don't have any religious beliefs, a 'faith' as such. So I'm unsure whether there really is a supernatural world beyond this one. I think there probably is. But I wouldn't like to actually say, 'Yes, I firmly believe; yes, this is where I stake my claim.' I'm sitting on the fence, hedging my bets."

Gittens publishes a journal, *For the Blood Is the Life,* which, in addition to featuring articles, allows members to express their thoughts about vampires. "One of the questions I ask in the new members' questionnaire is, have they ever thought they would like to be a vampire?" he said. "I get the occasional person who says this sounds like an offer, and yes, please. I'm trying to find people's motivations for joining groups like mine. This is my attempt at amateur psychology—I'm not trying to propose that we all get ourselves together and get made into the walking dead. The idea of it happening to me would frighten the life out of me. I'm a vegetarian, and my God, they want blood!"

"What do you see are the influences on these fantasies?" I asked.

"A lot of people read Anne Rice. People concentrate on the supposedly romantic aspects of the legend. They have taken the Christopher Lee–Frank Langella image of Count Dracula as being a tall, handsome, and distinguished chap in elegant clothes, the type of foreign nobleman with all this strength and elegance—the superficial drama of the character as portrayed in the cinema. You get a lot of people going around with white-painted faces, dyed black hair, the long black coats, the whole vampiric image. They think it's a very glamorous thing to be."

Gittens said he had been contacted by several individuals who claim to be vampires. Among them was Damien (see Chapter Two), whom Gittens considers vampiric, or vampirelike. Another was a woman who used the pseudonym "Ilona." Ilona wrote letters about her vampirism. She impressed Gittens as a loner whose story was "a pretty good in joke," as he put it. "She's kept it up to this day, for three years. We're not in regular contact anymore, but I know who she is and where she is. I've never met her, but I've talked to her on the telephone. She told me once in one of her letters that she was this supernatural being, that she's lived since Victorian times, that she was over a hundred years old, that she only went out at night. Much of what she told me came straight out of *Interview with the Vampire*. She writes in this pseudo-Gothic script, very flowing. Judging from inconsistencies in it, it is obviously not her natural handwriting. She gave me an address and a name that I was to send replies to. I checked those against the phone book and found that it was a real address and a real person. One Saturday I rang the number and talked to Ilona—*in the middle of the afternoon*—[yet] she claims she only gets up at night. She was a young woman with a slight hangover and a heavy smoker's cough. She still claimed that she was a vampire, and that she had the curtains drawn to protect herself from the sunlight."

Was her story a hoax that she was trying to perpetrate, or was it her explanation of her own Vampire Reality? Gittens told me he didn't know. We went on to discuss other cases.

"There are people in London who call themselves vampires," said Gittens. "I wouldn't go so far as to say they're an organized coven. They regularly get stitched up by the popular press, who write hideous articles about them."

Few letter-writers have caused him problems, he said. "I can cope with the occasional slightly eccentric person who wants information on where to locate vampire gravesites because he wants to be a vampire or to do away with them. We get those who are fanatically antivampire and those who are fanatically provampire. People want to be junior Sean Manchesters [one of England's vampire hunters—see Chapter Five] or mini–Christopher Lees. The majority are in the middle of those extremes and their interest is less obsessive."

"How do you respond to the would-be vampire hunters?" I asked him.

"Usually they're already in touch with Manchester, and I tell them that he's the man to talk to. I explain to these people that I'm a writer and a researcher and am trying to understand the vampire to my own personal satisfaction and pass on what I learn. I don't do fieldwork."

The Dracula Society, cofounded by Bernard Davies

in 1973 in London, was formed strictly for adult fans of horror literature. The same year, Davies created the first "Dracula tour," taking people around the Romanian countryside to visit places where Stoker had placed action. With its focus on film and literature, the Dracula Society attracts few want-to-be vampires. The desire to be a vampire mystifies Davies, who, as we saw in the previous chapter, points out quite eloquently that there is nothing romantic about folkloric vampirism.

Davies is forthright with his opinions and pulls no punches, I learned during our afternoon together. It was another hot day in London. We strolled along the Serpentine in Hyde Park, settled beneath the shade of an enormous tree for a while, and then adjourned to tea and scones at the lakeside café. It was a Friday afternoon and the park was filled with people. I was startled to see a number of men stretched out on the grass here and there clad only in bikini underwear, their conservative business suits folded neatly in piles beside them. Apparently in cloudy but merry old England, one takes the sun when and where one finds it.

"Some of the explanations for vampires are so farfetched and are scientifically unsound," Davies said. "When I talk about real vampirism, I don't mean pseudovampirism, the kind of thing that is very popular in the States. Those people are, as far as I'm concerned, a load of kooks. Anyone who thinks he needs blood to live is just a little bit weird. But then, weird philosophies are very popular over there in the States, aren't they, and it's only a matter of time before they come over here. These blood-drinkers are just people, not vampires. To be a vampire, you have to be *dead* first."

However, Davies agreed that real vampires might exist, either as self-induced phenomena based on strong belief, or in terms of external beings perceived by psychic senses. "It's an open question," he said. "The mind has strange powers, and we don't know enough about it. There is an actuality about such supernatural experiences and I don't pooh-pooh them. If you believe that such experiences are possible, there's nothing particularly strange about real vampires. You can accept them. There are plenty of well-accredited instances of people having encounters with entities who have attacked them and thrown them about with physical force. If you can say that kind of entity might exist, then the possibility of it assuming a vampire form is not impossible to accept at all.

"If you're a good Christian and believe in the authority of the Bible, then you accept that Christ died and then rose in solid form. You could call him vampiroid, for want of a better term. What forces were called into play to enable him to do that, we don't know. But very similar forces affect other persons deceased. If you can accept one, why can't you accept the other? I have no desire to offend pious Christians," Davies hastened to add, perhaps already seeing indignant and scorching letters from the holy piling up in the post. "I was raised one myself. But you have to accept what the Bible says, and it's a perfect description of a quasi-vampire experience. Not a malign one, but a benign one."

Davies is quick to dismiss Freudian interpretations of vampires. "I don't accept this craven worship of everything having to do with Freud that Americans seem to have, especially Americans who write about myth and magic. I think a great deal of Freud's work has been devalued in recent times—a lot of Freud's bluff has been blown. He has been shown to have devised a great number of accretions around so-called results of his work that aren't valid at all, and have a lot to do with the peculiarities of his own mind.

"One cannot apply Freudian psychoanalytical explanations to things that people claim they experience. And you cannot apply Freud to people in a different era and context from Freud's. You cannot use Freudian psychoanalysis to analyze the experiences of mid-European, illiterate peasants in the fifteenth to seventeenth centuries who were living close to the soil. Those worlds were so vastly different that if we were to meet people from them, including our own ancestors, we shouldn't understand a thing they were talking about. And they wouldn't understand us. Their experience, their view of the world, their whole moral, religious, and psychic parameters were totally different from ours. Even a generation or two makes a great gap in people. We know that generations hence things will happen that we can't conceive now. Our great-grandfathers couldn't conceive of taking a heart out of a dead person and giving it to somebody else. That belonged to the realm of Mary Shelley."

Like some others who have studied psychic phenomena, Davies theorizes that in earlier centuries, psychic and mediumistic abilities were much more common, and probably were shared collectively in villages. With such a communal psychic force, he said, it would not be unusual for more than one person to see the walking dead, and in a form that appeared physical and real.

I asked him what he thought Bram Stoker believed. Did the man who ignited the modern fascination with vampires believe in them himself?

"What Stoker believed about vampires, I do not know," Davies replied. "But he was very keen on everything to do with the supernatural from his boyhood. When he was a young man, I'd say college-age, he knew Hamilton Dean's mother, and they would often talk for hours about mythology and superstitions. I think these things fascinated Bram his whole life."

In earlier times, the vampire was a terrible, loathsome creature that reminded humankind of its fear of death and of the dead returning. The vampire was the remnant of a human being, something gone haywire. Its essential humanness, however, has enabled us to reinvent it over passing generations. Literary invention has made the vampire less monstrous and more like us. It is still a repository of fears and anxieties but has acquired an exotic aura. The vampire exists in the forbidden zone of the human psyche, beckoning us even as it repels us. The modern vampire has become our antidote and answer for our feelings of loneliness, isolation, and alienation, for our fears of death and sexual and personal intimacy, for romantic fantasies, blood cravings, sexual tastes, the desire to be trendy, and the need to be noticed.

Although we've glamorized the vampire, we still believe in the vampire of yore, the awful being who haunts graveyards and occupies an uncorrupt corpse. When the possibility of such a vampire is raised, vampire hunters respond with stake and hammer.

Chapter Five

Stalking the Vampire

IN 1970, A FUROR ERUPTED OVER THE ALLEGED EXISTENCE of a vampire in London's Highgate Cemetery. Numerous people attested to seeing a menacing creature drifting about the perimeter of the grounds at night. It was subsequently identified as a vampire—an Undead corpse that rose from its grave at night. There was a splash in the press, which incited a small army of self-styled vampire hunters and thrill seekers to descend upon the cemetery at night. Graves were vandalized and corpses were desecrated, and access to the cemetery was soon restricted.

One individual emerged as vampire stalker supreme: Sean Manchester, president of an occult society, now defunct, which has as its still-active arms the Vampire Research Society and the International Society for the Advancement of Irreproducible Vampire and Lycanthropy Research (ISAIVLR). According to Manchester—now the Reverend Manchester—he succeeded in tracking the vampire to his lair in an abandoned mansion and, in the best East European tradition, drove a stake through its evil heart, causing a "terrible roar" to sound from "the bowels of hell."

The case became famous for its controversy. Some say there never was a vampire, though there may have been ghosts mistaken for vampires. Others say there was a vampire. Still others maintain there was a vampire, but that Sean Manchester didn't find it and the story of the staked vampire is not true. The mystery remains unsolved. But the case earned Reverend Manchester a place in the public eye as "vampire hunter general" and enemy of the forces of darkness. Because of the continuing interest and controversy in the Highgate vampire case, Manchester was one of those at the top of my list to seek out during my stay in England.

Before meeting Manchester, I paid a visit to Highgate Cemetery to familiarize myself with the terrain. If there is such a thing as the perfect vampire haunt, Highgate Cemetery is it. Bram Stoker apparently thought so, for the evidence points to him using Highgate as the model for the cemetery near Hampstead Heath where Lucy Westenra is buried in *Dracula*. Stoker didn't name Highgate, disguising it in his novel, but it is the only cemetery near Hampstead Heath that fits the description in the book. Perhaps *Dracula* is the source of later rumors about a vampire infestation in the real cemetery. Such rumors have no foundation, according to Bernard Davies, among the skeptics concerning the Highgate vampire case. Davies told me he had found no historical evidence prior to Stoker's time that associated Highgate Village or Highgate Cemetery with vampires.

The cemetery sits atop a hill in Highgate, one of London's northern neighborhoods. A sprawling place, it is divided into halves, cut through by Swains Lane. The eastern side is newer and still active, with several burials a week. Karl Marx, George Eliot, and Sir Ralph Richardson are buried there, among other luminaries. The markers are a mix of Victorian and modern. For a small fee, the public can enter during the day and wander freely along numerous narrow footpaths.

The western half, however, is closed to the public except on guided tours. It is the original cemetery, and is a jungle of brush, overgrowth, jumbled tombstones, and half-hidden vaults. Michael Faraday, Radclyffe Hall, and the wife and daughter of Charles Dickens are among its notable occupants. On the western side, one finds Victorian glorification of death at its peak. Winged angels and mournful animals watch over tombs. Crosses and fabulous crypts jut toward the sky. Vines cling to everything. The overgrowth makes the place dark even on a sunny day, and if the day is cloudy, it looks most gloomy and foreboding.

Highgate has a long and illustrious history. A hermitage existed there as early as 1364, and the wealthy began settling nearby during the sixteenth century. They were attracted by the stunning views of London, the Thames, and the Surrey hills—views partly obscured by urban growth today. By the late seventeenth century, Highgate was a village unto itself. One of the best-sited homes for the view was constructed on what is now part of the cemetery by William Ashurst, a merchant, member of Parliament, and lord mayor of Highgate. Ashurst died in 1720. In

1830, his house was pulled down to make way for St. Michael's Church.

By the 1820s, London faced a terrible problem. The city was growing fast, and there was nowhere to bury the dead. Some 52,000 people expired every year, and the church cemeteries were so overstuffed that they literally belched up their corpses. In answer to the dilemma, private cemeteries opened. This was nothing short of a revolution in burial practices, for private cemeteries were unheard-of. These profit-driven operations charged money for interment.

Highgate Cemetery was created by the London Cemetery Company. Stephen Geary, the architect and founder, set out to design and landscape the most spectacular cemetery in all of London to ensure its success. It would celebrate death in the darkest and grandest glory that Victorian art and architecture could muster. It was the Age of Romantic Antiquity and Gothic Revival. Geary acquired seventeen acres, including the Ashurst estate, and laid out systematic rows of graves. He planned for 30,000 graves, each containing three bodies.

His pièces de résistance were Egyptian Avenue and the Circle of Lebanon, also called the Columbarium. Egyptian Avenue was excavated into the steepest part of the hill; it is twelve feet below ground level. One approaches it through an iron gateway under massive Pharaonic arches flanked by obelisks. The sides of Egyptian Avenue, leading to the Circle of Lebanon, are lined with sixteen vaults, each of which holds twelve coffins. The Circle of Lebanon is a circle of twenty vaults, even more magnificent, dug thirty feet below ground level. In the center is a great cedar of

Lebanon, which had been part of the original Ashurst estate.

Near the circle are the Terrace Catacombs, an underground gallery with 840 recesses. Some 500 cholera victims are stuffed away in the left wing of the catacombs. St. Michael's Church faces the catacombs from across a street.

On May 20, 1839, the cemetery was consecrated by the Bishop of London. Two acres were left unhallowed for the burial of "dissenters"—agnostics, atheists, non-Anglicans, and the like. The first burial took place three days later, and Highgate became London's third commercial cemetery.

Highgate quickly became one of the most sought-after resting places in London. A modest grave cost £2 10 shillings (the shilling was worth five of today's pence). Interment in the Circle of Lebanon cost 200 guineas, (£210)—a phenomenal sum of money for the times. Money talked—fame, social prominence, and bloodlines had nothing to do with the grandeur of one's grave. Some of the most imposing vaults and markers were purchased by persons of no historical importance. The first year the cemetery was in operation, 204 people were buried there. Most of them were from London and were an average age of thirty-six. The living, meanwhile, flocked to Highgate to be seen, promenading past St. Michael's Church and the Terrace Catacombs on pleasant days.

Business was so good that in 1854, the company purchased an additional nineteen acres to expand to the east side. Geary died the same year and was buried on the west side.

By World War I, however, the cemetery was in

decline. The London Cemetery Company was taken over by United Cemeteries Limited. Fewer families bought plots, and many of those that did failed to maintain them. Following World War II, the decline accelerated. The cemetery, especially the western side, was engulfed by brush and rapidly growing sycamore trees. The overgrowth choked pathways and the sycamore roots split vaults, causing shanks of marble to tilt at crazy angles. Graves sank and some opened, only to be covered over by a mask of brush. The unwary visitor could not only lose his way, he could lose his footing and fall into a thirty-foot-deep ruptured vault. The only creatures happy with this state of affairs were the foxes, badgers, hedgehogs, squirrels, birds, rodents, and other creatures who lived relatively undisturbed amidst the clutter.

On my first visit to Highgate, I took the tube to Archway and then labored on foot up steep Highgate Hill to the cemetery. The neighborhood is working-class now, an ethnic mix. The red brick row houses lining the street looked somber under an overcast sky. Partway up, I cut over to Swains Lane, which took me through the heart of the cemetery. In Victorian times, horse-drawn hearses pulled up the lane to the cemetery gates, west side on the left and east side across the lane on the right. To minimize obstruction to traffic on the lane, the coffins were taken out and lowered by hydraulic lift to a tunnel underneath the road. They would be raised and lifted out on the cemetery grounds.

I took a self-guided tour of the east side and signed up for the next available guided tour of the west side. At the appointed hour, about half a dozen people were collected. We were greeted by a small old man dressed in a baggy green sweater and slacks with brown wool socks and brown sandals. He had a bushy head of long gray and white hair and an equally bushy beard to match. For the next hour or so, he kept us entertained with his droll sense of humor.

We were advised to keep strictly to the footpaths to avoid treacherous hidden graves and vaults.

We learned that the east side once again has become a fashionable burying ground; plots are purchased by individuals as young as twenty-one. The west side is so full of bodies that practically every square inch of ground covers a grave. One can be buried here only if a family vault already exists. In all, Highgate contains some 60,000 vaults and 170,000 bodies.

Any graveyard has a psychic atmosphere that differs from that of the surrounding world of the living. There probably isn't a graveyard in existence where ghosts and unexplained phenomena haven't been reported. Highgate was not a place where I would have wanted to be caught after dark.

Egyptian Avenue and the Circle of Lebanon were dark and gloomy. This part of Highgate has been made famous on film and television, for this is where studios, production companies, and television crews come whenever they need to shoot a vampire's lair. Hammer Films was here in the 1950s through early 1970s for its famous Dracula films starring Christopher Lee and Peter Cushing. The Friends of Highgate now charge hefty fees for the privilege of shooting the funereal scenery. "What would we do without our vampires and Dracula?" said our guide. "Dracula is big business!"

Many tourists come to Highgate expecting Count Dracula himself to be buried here. Our puckish guide said he grew so weary of being asked for directions to Dracula's grave that he began telling tourists that the Count was really buried under Platform Five at the Kings Cross Underground/British Rail station in London. "One American girl actually went there looking for the grave," he said. "She came back quite peeved. She said the least they could do was put a plaque on the platform!"

I asked the guide if Highgate Cemetery was haunted.

"Of *course* it's haunted," he said. "We've got *everything* here." Many visitors report seeing apparitions, and a number of the volunteer staff, who all spend a great deal of time prowling about the pathways alone, also say they see ghosts. In the typical English fashion of understatement, these experiences are not trumpeted about but are kept private. Ask about them, however, and they are acknowledged.

"What about the Highgate vampire?" I asked.

The guide scowled. "Don't tell me you've read *that* book." He was referring to the infamous book by Sean Manchester, *The Highgate Vampire* (1985), which purports to tell the full and unexpurgated account of the vampire reportedly haunting the cemetery in the 1970s. "Complete rubbish and utter nonsense," the guide snorted. And with that, the subject of real vampires at Highgate was dismissed.

My next opportunity to discuss the Highgate vampire came several days later, when I returned to Highgate to meet with Sean Manchester and his executive secretary, Diana Brewster. Our rendezvous took place at the Lauderdale House, a historical site with a small café located on Highgate Hill adjacent to Waterlow Park and the cemetery. The location was Manchester's choice, despite the fact that the Friends of Highgate Cemetery had pressured the Lauderdale House to discontinue selling *The Highgate Vampire* in its bookshop. The three of us sat outdoors under a blistering sun and talked over cappuccino and strawberries.

Manchester, handsome and genial, was attired in a cassock. He explained that he was about to be ordained as a priest by the Celtic Catholic Church, which is independent of the Vatican. He has his own order, the Holy Grail Church.

Manchester has always cultivated a striking Romantic appearance in haircut and period clothing, perhaps to underscore his claim to blood lineage to one of the greatest Romantic poets, Lord Byron. The lineage cannot be proved, according to Manchester, because it is through the illegitimate offspring of a liaison between Byron and a household servant. Nonetheless, he wears this badge proudly, and has often been featured in the press dressed in Byronic attire. The Byron Society says it cannot comment on his claim of lineage since no written evidence of it exists, and notes only that many similar claims are made by others.

Manchester said he grew up in Newstead Abbey Park in Sherwood Forest, Nottinghamshire, some distance from Newstead Abbey, a converted twelfth-century priory that was home to the family of Lord Byron from 1540 until 1817, when the poet was forced to sell it to pay debts. The house was restored in the Gothic style in the nineteenth century and is a museum today. This environment, a "time capsule untouched by centuries," as Manchester described it, predisposed him to an early interest in the supernatural. He said he detested formal education and ran away at age fifteen without ever having taken a single exam. His true teacher was nature, and he devoted himself to his own pursuit of poetry, music, and painting. "I've always been a bit of a bohemian, a bit of a poet, a bit of a wandering minstrel," he said in answer to a question as to how he earned his living in his pre-vampire-hunting days. "The Grail quest, the discovery of one's true self, has been my main drive through life. That I have slain dragons and rescued maidens has been along the way. I have never been occupied in a nine-to-five office job simply because I don't think I'm capable of it. My abilities are more tied up with my quests. Sometimes it's not made it easy because of not having a solid, reliable income. But of course one learns to live as someone on a spiritual journey should. Sometimes it will be difficult, other times you don't notice those difficulties. It does come to you. I'm always looked after, wherever I go."

Thus, when the vampire surfaced at Highgate, Manchester answered the call to rescue maidens and slay the vampire-dragon.

Reports of a vampire at Highgate first came to light in 1967. The story, which unfolded over several years, is marked by ambiguities, weird activities, and claims that are backed up by questionable evidence. Highly entertaining, the case, even at its best, can strain one's credulity. The most complete accounts have been given by Manchester in two major works: a chapter in

The Vampire's Bedside Companion (1975), edited by Peter Underwood, founder of the eminent Ghost Club in England, and *The Highgate Vampire,* a book that Manchester self-published in 1985 and revised in 1990. Manchester's chapter in Underwood's book gives a straightforward account of various reports of the vampire, and his own identification of the corpse believed to be the Undead one. His second account, *The Highgate Vampire,* expands the story and includes Manchester's tracking the vampire to a new lair, where he spectacularly dispatched it.

The story is recounted here from Manchester's writings and a number of newspaper reports and periodical articles.

The Haunting of Highgate

The first reports of something foul afoot in Highgate came from two sixteen-year-old girls who shared a terrifying vision one night while walking home down Swains Lane. As they passed the rusted and locked north gate of the western side of the cemetery, they both saw graves open and dead bodies rise from them. The vision ended as soon as they spoke to each other. One of the girls, Elizabeth Wojdyla, then began suffering nightmares in which an evil presence with a pale, corpselike face was trying to enter her bedroom.

Several weeks later, a young man and his girlfriend experienced a fright while walking down Swains Lane at night. As they passed the north gate, the girl suddenly screamed. They both saw a figure standing behind the iron railings of the gate. Its face was twisted into a mask of horror. They froze and watched the figure melt back into the shadows of the cemetery.

When Manchester heard the second account, he decided to investigate. He was as yet unaware of the experience of the two girls. He poked about the western side during the day, and noticed that a path from the unused northern gate led directly to the Columbarium. But the young man who'd reported the incident refused Manchester's request to meet him at the cemetery for a night visit. He told Manchester that he had returned to the cemetery with another friend one night near midnight. They'd climbed the wall near the north gate and moved deeper into the grounds. They were startled by a deep, slow booming sound that came closer and closer, until a dark shape moved across the path directly in front of them. Terrified, they fled.

The mysterious figure remained unexplained, and little else happened for nearly two and a half years. During the summer of 1969, Manchester had a chance meeting with Wojdyla, who by this time was so thin and pale that she looked like a cadaver. She told him of her nightmares, headaches, dizziness, and nausea. She had bouts of sleepwalking as well.

Soon after this meeting, Wojdyla's boyfriend, Keith, contacted Manchester for help, explaining that a doctor's regimen of diet and vitamins had failed to improve her condition. In addition to her other symptoms, she now showed two small puncture wounds on her neck, Keith reported. Manchester suggested she was under attack by a vampire. He and Keith sealed her room with garlic and a crucifix and gave her a silver cross to wear, along with a necklace made of linen containing a small amount of salt. Keith was to take other measures of prayer and the sprinkling of holy water about the room. Following these steps, Wojdyla's health improved.

Manchester and several unidentified colleagues began inquiring into phenomena experienced in the cemetery area. Perhaps because of their inquiries, numerous reports were offered. It appears that the reports snowballed to the point where the local press took notice in February 1970 by reporting some of them. Numerous people claimed to have seen a ghostly figure lurking about the area. One young man claimed to have been knocked down by a tall figure with the face of a wild animal.

The reports included no evidence of vampirism, however. Meanwhile, dead animals, mostly foxes and other nocturnal creatures, began to appear in Waterlow Park and the cemetery. They were all lacerated around the throat and drained of blood. Manchester opined publicly that the culprit of all the strange events was a vampire that should be dispatched in the traditional manner by staking it through the heart and beheading the corpse. When his remarks appeared in the press, the entire affair mushroomed. Others expressed doubt over the vampire theory. One alternative theory held that the caretaker's dog had killed the animals and dragged them about, thus draining them of their blood. But the idea of a vampire loose in Highgate caught the public's fancy, and hordes of vampire hunters and the curious invaded the cemetery.

One of the many who contacted Manchester was the sister of a woman he calls "Lusia." Lusia reportedly was suffering from somnambulism, feelings of suffocation at night, and other odd behavior. She had two tiny pinprick marks on her neck. One night as the sleepwalking Lusia headed toward Highgate Cemetery, the sister, Anne, rang Manchester. The two of them trailed Lusia to St. Michael's Church, through a broken railing of the west-side cemetery boundary, and to the Columbarium. There Lusia stopped before one of the vaults and ripped the crucifix from about her neck. A low booming sound echoed through the area. Lusia collapsed. Anne and Manchester carried her home. She had no recollection of the event the next morning.

Meanwhile, public interest reached fever pitch following a show broadcast by Thames Television, in which Manchester led an interviewer on a tour of the vault area where the suspected vampire was said to lurk. Other vampire hunters announced their intent to find the vampire and stake it. One of them was David Farrant, born David Robert Donovan Farrant, who gave his name at various times as David Farrant, Allan Farrant, and Robert Farrant. Farrant, a young man who lived in the Highgate area, inspired numerous other would-be vampire hunters to climb the cemetery walls and invade the grounds. Farrant claimed to have seen a strange shape on four occasions during his own nocturnal forays. The eight-foot, humanoid shape glided over ground where, Farrant believed, vaults had been newly damaged.

Some of the sightings may have natural explanations, however. At about the same time, a group of amateur filmmakers was working in the cemetery filming *Vampires at Night,* and it is possible that some of the "shapes" floating about were real human beings in costume. But Farrant clung to his belief that he had encountered a true supernatural entity.

Meanwhile, Manchester continued his own activities. On Friday night, March 13, 1970, he led a group of about a hundred people to the vault singled out by Lusia. The iron door would not open, so Manchester and two assistants lowered themselves into the tomb from a hole in the top of the Circle of Lebanon, which forms an earthly roof over the vaults of the inner circle. Inside the vault they found three empty coffins. In each of them they placed garlic, salt, and a cross, and they sprinkled the coffins and the vault with holy water. They left the tomb and stood watch for the night. At about 2 AM, the booming noise sounded again. (The source of this mysterious noise was never explained, but we may presume it was associated with the vampire.)

The news media continued to report stories of sightings of menacing, ghostly figures in the cemetery. In August 1970, the situation worsened. The mutilated corpse of a woman buried in the cemetery forty-four years earlier was discovered beside a broken vault. The corpse was charred and missing the head and an arm. There was evidence that an occult ritual had taken place. It was speculated that the abuse had been perpetrated by a zealous vampire hunter or by satanists.

Disturbed by the desecration of the corpse, Manchester returned to the Columbarium and lowered himself into the suspect vault. One of the three coffins was missing. He then contacted Lusia and convinced her to return with him to the site during daylight hours. They were accompanied by three assistants. Seated in front of the vault, Lusia entered a trance and seemed to become an instrument for an evil entity. She answered questions put by Manchester, then walked to a nearby vault and began crying. It was the vault where the headless woman's corpse had been interred.

Manchester wondered if the vampire had changed lairs since the purification of the suspect vault. The doors of this vault yielded to pressure. Inside, Manchester, his assistants, and Lusia were greeted with a revolting stench and decaying coffins. They noticed that the vault contained one coffin too many, according to the inscriptions on the outside of the vault. Was it the missing coffin from the other vault? Perhaps. They identified the extra coffin as one in the back that appeared newer than the others and had no nameplate. With pounding hearts, they raised the lid.

Accounts of what they found inside differ. Manchester said in his first account in *The Vampire's Bedside Companion:*

> There it lay: a body which appeared neither dead nor alive. Eerily, we gazed at that sight which defied explanation and logic for several long moments. "It's newly dead," said one of my assistants, breaking the silence. But the vault was a hundred years old and there had been no recent admissions.

Ten years later, in his unexpurgated and expanded account in *The Highgate Vampire,* the description was much more vivid:

> My torch lit up in unnerving revelation the sleeping form of something that had long been dead; something

nevertheless gorged and stinking with the life-blood of others, fresh clots of which still adhered to the edge of the mouth whose fetid breath made me sick to my stomach. The glazed eyes stared horribly—almost mocking me, almost knowing that my efforts to destroy it would be thwarted. Under the parchment-like skin a faint bluish tinge could be detected. The face was the colour and appearance of a three-day-old corpse.

The group stared at the thing in horror for some minutes; then Manchester took from his bag of holy tricks an aspen stake and placed it on the breast of the vampire. His assistants exhorted him to desist, because staking the body would be an illegal desecration of a corpse. Manchester relented and agreed to perform an exorcism instead with garlic, salt, holy water, incense, candles, crosses, and incantations intended to banish the evil forever. The group had to hurry, for the sun was near setting. As the rite proceeded, the temperature plunged and the candles flickered. The eerie booming noise sounded. At the end of the rite, Manchester hurled a crucifix into the vault.

Later, upon Manchester's recommendation, he said, the entrance to the vault was sealed with cement. (In his second account, Manchester said that garlic was mixed into the cement.)

Despite the exorcism, Manchester considered the case open until the vampire was properly dispatched. The exorcism might have allayed the fears of some, as Manchester asserted, but not Farrant. On August 29, on the night of the full moon, the police arrested Farrant as he climbed over the Highgate Cemetery wall with a wooden cross and a sharp wooden stake in hand. Farrant identified himself as Allan Farrant, an orderly at Barnet General Hospital. He admitted he was out to stake the vampire, which he believed had haunted the cemetery for about ten years. He was charged with entering enclosed premises for an unlawful purpose, but the charges were dismissed in court. Farrant stated he had formed an organization several years earlier that had about a hundred members throughout Britain and Europe who were stalking vampires.

Nearly one month later, Farrant was back in the press, this time as David Farrant, leading a reporter on a tour of the cemetery, again armed with cross and stake. This time, Farrant hid his tools in a paper bag. They found no vampire, but did find extensive, recent desecration throughout the cemetery. Graves and coffins had been opened and their contents moved or stolen, and vaults had been defaced with occult symbols. The damage was estimated at £10,000, a staggering sum at the time. The public was outraged.

Farrant kept a nightly vigil at the cemetery for a while, and though he never saw the specter nor found the vampire, he did not give up on his mission.

Throughout 1971, there were periodic reports of occult activities taking place in the cemetery during the night. Farrant surfaced once again in the news when he was apprehended by police on the night of October 8, 1971, while in the company of a naked woman. The two allegedly were photographing magical ceremonies, possibly necromancy, which is the conjuring of the dead for prophecy. Farrant said he was "high priest" of an occult order founded by Manchester. He was released from custody.

Manchester denied any association with Farrant.

Meanwhile, Manchester pursued his own investigations. Lusia, in trance, told him that the vampire in Highgate Cemetery had succeeded in moving to a new location. Manchester had the first vault reopened. He found that the casket that he believed held the elusive Undead one was missing—and so were the garlic, crucifixes, and bags of salt he had left there.

In the winter of 1973, a deserted nineteenth-century mansion in north London surfaced in the media as reportedly haunted by something so unpleasant that local people called it the "House of Dracula." Manchester decided to investigate. He took with him two assistants, a clairvoyant woman named Veronika and a "skeptic" named Arthur, who would operate "the scientific equipment." Entering the house at night, they had a number of harrowing experiences involving a sinister fog, terrible smells, icy presences, knocking noises, and voices heard only by Veronika. They determined that they had found the lair of the escaped Undead. Arthur and Manchester returned in daylight to stake the vampire.

In the basement they found an enormous black casket. They dragged it outside to the rear of the house grounds. According to *The Highgate Vampire:*

Arthur rushed to fetch my case of stakes as I prayed for strength. Suddenly I kicked the lid off the coffin and beheld something which shall ever remain stained upon my memory. In the half-light our quarry looked fiendishly exaggerated and distorted—much worse than the time before in the vault at Highgate. Burning, fierce eyes beneath black furrowed brows stared with hellish reflection. Yellow at the edges with blood-red centres, they were unlike any other beast of prey.

Flared nostrils connected to a thin, high-bridged nose. The mouth still set in its cruel expression with lips drawn far back as if unable to contain the fangs. The creature had not long entered its vampire sleep and the hideous countenance was yet to become subdued by its undead repose.

The vampire's skin began to discolor immediately from the sunlight coming through the overhead tree branches, Manchester said. And then:

> With a mighty blow I drove the stake through the creature's heart, then shielded my ears as a terrible roar emitted from the bowels of hell. This died away as suddenly as it had erupted and all became still. We witnessed the body-shell cave in and quickly turn filthy brown which soon became a sluggish flow of inhuman slime and viscera in the bottom of the casket. Arthur had been trying to use a camera as if he could not believe his eyes, but the intolerably putrid stench soon caused him to turn away nauseated.

Manchester and Arthur then built a pyre, placed the coffin and its awful contents on top, poured on gasoline, and lit it. The vampire's remains burned to ash.

The house later was razed, and flats for the elderly were erected upon the grounds.

But Highgate Cemetery still was not at rest. Graves were tampered with, bodies were taken out of coffins, and occult symbols were written on vault floors and walls. In January 1974, a hapless architect parked his car near the cemetery one night, and the next morning found what at first appeared to be a log resting in the seat. It was a headless corpse. Sometime later, Farrant was again apprehended by police, who took from him photos of a nude woman dancing in a tomb. He was arrested and charged with grave despoliation, illegal possession of a handgun, and petty theft.

Farrant was brought to trial in Central Criminal Court in June 1974, in what was called the "Nude Rituals Case." It was juicy stuff for the media, and the trial was widely covered. Interest was fueled by the fact that prior to the commencement of the trial, Farrant and a codefendant, John Pope, allegedly sent poppets stuck with pins to the detectives who intended to testify at the trial. The poppets, small dolls used as effigies in magical rituals, apparently represented the detectives and were intended as a warning not to testify.

The trial proceeded, and Farrant conducted his own defense. He pleaded not guilty to five charges, including one charge of damaging a memorial to the dead on consecrated grounds, one charge of damaging property, and three charges of breaking open catacombs and interfering with corpses. He also denied practicing necromantic rituals in vaults at Highgate. The incident that was the basis of that charge had been a satanic ritual performed by other persons, he said, and his own group had performed an exorcism that involved the dancing nude woman. Farrant did plead guilty to possessing a revolver and one round of ammunition.

The prosecution contended that the offenses took place over a three-year period, and that Farrant was the true "vampire" of Highgate. The jury was shown photographs, alleged to have been found in Farrant's home, of a desecrated coffin, occult symbols in a vault, and a nude woman dancing inside a vault. Among those who testified was author Francis King, an authority on magic, who said that the occult symbols on the floor of a vault at Highgate were those used in necromancy.

Farrant was convicted and was sentenced in July 1974 to four years and eight months in jail, plus a fine of £750 to cover court costs. In passing sentence, the judge noted that tomb desecration was still occurring at the cemetery, for he had gone to Highgate the day before to see a mutilated corpse inside a damaged coffin. At the sentencing, the judge heard testimony from John Duncan Kidd, a solicitor and a director of United Cemeteries Ltd., the owner of Highgate Cemetery. Kidd stated that the cost of cleaning up Highgate was "absolutely phenomenal" and would exceed the cemetery's limited income and subsidy from the parent company.

In two other trials, Farrant was convicted of interfering with witnesses to a criminal trial—the poppet incident—and of stealing blankets and bed linen from Barnet General Hospital.

In October 1975, the Friends of Highgate Cemetery was formed, partly in response to outrage over the occult activities. The purpose of the Friends was to manage Highgate Cemetery as a national monument and historical burial ground, to represent the interests of grave owners, to secure public access to the grounds, and to sponsor conservation of the cemetery. The Friends formed a volunteer maintenance squad, which began hacking away at the overgrowth, felling some of the sycamores, clearing the paths, and restoring the place to at least some of its former eminence. They didn't overdo the clearing—the place, after all, had to maintain its famous "Victorian gloom." To discourage occult activity and vandalism, the cemetery was closed at night and access to the west side was severely restricted. In 1981, two Friends formed Pinemarsh Limited and bought Highgate Cemetery, east and west sides, for a mere £50.

Farrant was released from jail on parole in July 1976.

In 1977, a rash of animal deaths began to be reported in the areas near Highgate Cemetery. The bodies of pets and various small wild animals were found with wounds in their throats. It was speculated that dogs or wild animals were the culprits, but the vampire theory also began to circulate again. For Manchester, there was only one possible explanation: The vampire he had destroyed had somehow managed to leave behind a new Undead.

By 1979, he learned that Lusia had died and was buried in the Great Northern London Cemetery, where sightings of a woman in white and other supernatural activities were being reported. Manchester concluded that Lusia had been contaminated by the vampire. He kept vigil at her gravesite to confirm this, and then one night cast a protective magic circle and performed an exorcism ritual.

What manifested was a hissing black spider the size of a full-grown cat, according to Manchester. He plunged a stake into it, whereupon it emitted a "heartrending screech." When dawn came, Manchester found the decomposing body of Lusia where the spider had met its demise. He reburied her. That, he said, finally laid to rest the vampiric activity at Highgate.

Farrant, however, was not done with vampires. In late 1986, he challenged Manchester to a duel. According to Manchester, the two met but no duel ever took place, and he then lost track of Farrant. Because Farrant had claimed to be the "high priest" of Manchester's organization, Manchester said, he dismantled the society and focused his efforts on the Vampire Research Society and the ISAIVLR. Once open to public membership, the ISAIVLR may now be joined by invitation only. The move was made in response to what Manchester termed "infiltration and abuse of information and research material" by unfriendly agents.

In representing the ISAIVLR, Manchester occasionally uses the pseudonym "Ruthwen Glenarvon." The name is taken from Byronic associations: Lord Ruthven is the vampire in John Polidori's story borrowed from Lord Byron's writings (see Chapter Four), and Glenarvon is the name of one of Byron's fictional characters. Ruthwen Glenarvon is listed as the editor of *The Cross and the Stake*, the newsletter of the ISAIVLR. According to Manchester, the name is used to answer correspondence and protect identities of various staff of the society. He has used it for some years (and, during the Highgate vampire case, he used the pseudonym "George Byron" while investigating the cemetery where Lusia was said to be buried).

Robin Hood: Highwayman Turned Vampire?

Vampires—or at least, headline-producing vampires —have been few and far between since the Highgate case vaulted Manchester to fame. He cited two other cases of possible vampirism that he has investigated: the Kirklees vampire and Lady Caroline Lamb, a lover of Lord Byron. Both are weak on vampire evidence and both are inconclusive.

Manchester said he had been researching the Lamb case for about ten years. "Ever since her death there has been talk of her passion living beyond the grave," he said. "There is an inkling of material to point to a vampiric side to it. She was clearly a disturbed personality who died brokenhearted and insane." He hastened to add, "There is *no* evidence that she was involved in the dark arts. Yet she set in force such powerful energies that they might well have remained after her death. Her distressed energy form has been seen and felt in Hertfordshire and other areas. There also has been a strange history in the same areas of something manifestly dark and vampiric. I don't know if the two are in any way connected. After ten years, that link has not been established beyond a reasonable doubt."

The Kirklees case likewise is slim on evidence. It concerns an alleged gravesite of the legendary figure Robin Hood and speculations on whether or not Robin Hood died the victim of a vampire—and thus may have become a vampire himself.

According to legend, Robin Hood, the thirteenth-century highwayman who robbed the rich and gave to the poor, was ill and distempered by the time he reached about fifty. He set off for the Kirklees priory to be treated by the prioress there, who was reputed to be skilled in the arts of "physique and surgery." En route, he was cursed by a witch. When he reached the nunnery, the prioress bled him and, because she felt him to be an enemy of the church, allowed him to bleed straight on to death. By other accounts, Robin Hood survived the bloodletting but was killed in a sword fight by Red Roger, who may have been Sir Roger of Doncaster. This same Sir Roger, according to yet other accounts, may have incited the prioress to dispatch Robin Hood. Before he expired, Robin Hood is said to have shot an arrow through the priory window to mark his grave. Because he was a highwayman, he was buried outside of consecrated ground near the priory. The alleged site—no one knows for certain that Robin Hood is buried there—is marked by a deteriorating monument that was rebuilt in the eighteenth century. The gravesite has been on private property almost since 1539, when Henry VIII broke with the Catholic Church and dissolved the monasteries and nunneries. It now belongs to Lady Margarete Armytage, the owner of Kirklees Hall estate, and is inaccessible. Allegedly, an exhumation was performed about 200 years ago, and the grave supposedly was found to be empty.

The notion that vampirism was involved in the legend of Robin Hood apparently never occurred to anyone for several centuries, until Manchester suggested it as a possibility to Barbara Green, president of the Yorkshire Robin Hood Society. Green met Manchester about four or five years ago, and he generously offered to become the society's patron and promote its interests. When he later proposed the vampire theory concerning Robin Hood's death, "it seemed worth pursuing," Green told me in an interview. She emphasized that the idea is theory only.

Manchester told Green that a "Ruthwen Glenarvon" from the ISAIVLR surreptitiously visited the gravesite and found that "certain things could be vampiric," as Green put it. In 1989, the vampire theory began to circulate in the media. "Ruthwen Glenarvon" wrote to Lady Armytage asking for permission to visit the grave and to interview Lady Armytage, information about the alleged exhumation, permission to examine the contents of the grave, and permission to allow "an accredited investigator from our society to keep vigil nocturnally near the grave for several nights." Lady Armytage would have none of it. "I have taken my solicitor's advice and don't want anything to do with them," she told the press.

The Yorkshire Robin Hood Society backs the ISAIVLR, Green said. She said that she sought the help of the local clergy to obtain permission to visit the grave and perform a blessing over it, but the local clergy—and higher Church of England officials—declined to become involved. A local priest was initially sympathetic, but after visiting Lady Armytage backed off.

Lady Armytage reported to the media that the gravesite had been vandalized by culprits unknown. It is possible that the vampire publicity may have encouraged some occult thrill seekers.

Green, who lives in Brighouse about two miles from the gravesite, said that after the publicity stirred things up, she began suffering mysterious manifestations in her own home, which she thought might be associated with the "atmosphere of evil" pervading the gravesite. She would wake up in the night and sense a presence, as though something evil were trying to take her over. A young girl staying in the house said something came into her own room and frightened her. The girl moved out, and Green slept with the lights on for about a month. Green also started to receive "nasty letters" from occultists in London. She didn't read most of them, but burned them and poured holy water over them.

Green said that she and a small band of like-minded friends, dressed in period costumes from Robin Hood's day, sneaked to the gravesite in April 1990. Nearby they found the body of a goat with its throat torn open, which they took as another sign of something evil afoot. At the gravesite, they performed a blessing.

The Robin Hood vampire theory has been dismissed by most vampire experts as a reach. There are difficulties with it. To begin with, there is no proof that Robin Hood ever existed. Various historical figures have been put forth as the famed highwayman, but some historians believe the legend is a composite of a number of men.

If Robin Hood did exist, and he did go to a priory to seek medical treatment, there is nothing unusual in the fact that he was bled. It was standard medical treatment at the time (and was up to the nineteenth century), the prevailing notion being that the blood carried bad humors and poisons that were eliminated in the bloodletting. (The fact that many patients were so weakened by the loss of blood that they died was an unfortunate side-effect.) There is nothing in the recorded stories about Robin Hood's demise to suggest that the prioress was a vampire (the word *vampire* was unknown in England at the time) or that she was a vampirelike spirit of the dead. Nor is there any evidence to suggest that the prioress drank Robin Hood's blood—and even if she had, it wouldn't necessarily mean that she was a vampire. In short, there is no evidence suggesting any supernatural hanky-panky.

And there also is no proof that Robin Hood, if he existed, is buried in the grave at Kirklees. Although all the documents concerning him say he is buried at Kirklees, the specific gravesite is unproven. The Robin Hood Society in Nottingham steers tourists to another site that they say may be the grave of the legendary hero.

Nonetheless, "the only possible way of identifying Undead activity is surveillance," Manchester said. "A vigil has been denied us by Lady Armytage. Thus it does seem improbable that we will arrive at a satisfactory conclusion."

Besides vampires, Manchester has waged war against all forces of darkness, including satanists. He published his own account of his rescue from a satanic cult of a beautiful young woman, Sarah, whom he married in 1987. Together they work to build Manchester's lay order and to battle evil. As a priest, Manchester expects to be more effective against the dark forces, and more effective as an exorcist of demonic agencies.

Manchester has his own beliefs as to where vampires belong in the order of creation. He defines a vampire as a "demon" and sees vampirism as part of the larger menace of satanism. It is a view similar to the one held by medieval Inquisitors, who said that Satan, with God's permission, torments humankind and wreaks evil upon the world. "There is a direct corollary between the rise in the cult of satanism and the dark arts—witchcraft, necromancy, black magic—and the incredible resurgence of interest in recent years in vampirism and real vampires," he said.

He observed that satanism takes many forms, including devotion to "the dark arts." One did not have to worship Satan per se to become one of his infernal servants. He said that satanic cults attract recruits by holding out promises of cheating death through a vampire existence from the grave. But prior to death, the initiates are vampirized psychically of their will and energy through mind control and domination. "The satanists suck the vital streams of energy and in the end the blood of their victims," he said. "Whatever they are promised in these cults of the vampire, the actual result is death."

If the victims gain the favor of Satan prior to death, a grisly vampire existence ensues, according to Manchester. Their corpses become possessed by the forces of evil. "They become like animals with gnashing teeth," he said. "They become *demonic,* a malevolent force of evil that contaminates their material residue. That is why the vampire can leave its resting place without disturbing a single blade of grass. It isn't the corpse itself, it is a masquerading, demonic force that has the ability to shape-shift, alter, and deceive."

The demonic vampire force sustaining a corpse lives outside of time, Manchester said. That is how it is able to preserve the body until it is cast out, and then the body disintegrates to ashes.

He said that even people who merely want to become vampires, for whatever reason, invite this horrible fate. He expressed concern for those who join vampire fan clubs. "You only have to look at the new members sections and see what they're saying. Would they like to become vampires? Would they indeed! This is the folklore equivalent to opening the door and inviting the vampire in. You don't have to physically open a door. The mental door is the real door. Then the vampire can come in anytime he wants."

Manchester believes that the ranks of the Undead are swelling in response to a calling-in by Satan, who is gathering his forces for the final confrontation of the Apocalypse. The legions of Undead are lying dormant in graves, like radioactive canisters, waiting to "spill forth their poison and contaminate the earth." A few who are evoked in occult rituals manage to escape their graves, he said. The rest await Satan's clarion call to action. "They are the legacy of our own collective evil," he observed, echoing the theory that human-kind has the power to project the contents of its own collective unconscious into a form that appears tangible.

Manchester said he spends a lot of time fending off critics who dispute his story as told in *The Highgate Vampire*. The account is markedly different from the story that first appeared in *The Vampire's Bedside Companion,* and some find the blood-gorged, decomposing corpse and shrieking spider incredible. Manchester answers them thusly: "I am not interested in whether people believe in vampires or not. I wrote

The Highgate Vampire to relieve myself of a very large mailbag of pressure from people who were asking what had happened. They had read *The Vampire's Bedside Companion* and only had the beginning of the story."

I asked him why the two accounts differed dramatically in the descriptions of the vampire exposed in his coffin. Surely the details in the second account, such as the bloodstained mouth, the fetid breath, and the staring eyes, should have been included in the first account. Manchester said he had indeed included them, but his account had been "radically edited" for "legal reasons" by the publisher. However, I later had a chance to ask Peter Underwood, who had collected and edited the material for *The Vampire's Bedside Companion,* if Manchester's chapter had indeed been drastically edited. Underwood said that to the best of his recollection, the Highgate account had been published as Manchester had supplied it, "without any editing."

Manchester's critics also discount photographs of the alleged vampire that he published in *The Highgate Vampire.* Manchester said the photos were taken by his assistant, Arthur, moments before the corpse disintegrated. I'm not sure what a vampire corpse should look like, but I had to agree with the critics that the photos didn't convince me. Manchester asserted the photos were genuine, and observed that one couldn't expect to see the likes of Christopher Lee meeting his doom in a Hammer film.

Manchester's description of the vampire's last moments, when it decomposed instantly into "inhuman slime and viscera" may be unique in vampire records.

In searching through historical cases, I found none in which the corpse of a suspected vampire decomposed or disintegrated immediately upon being violated. The corpses were usually dismembered and burned. In film and literature, we find more theatrical demises. Stoker's Count Dracula—who is knifed to death in his box of earth, rather than staked in his coffin—crumbles to dust "almost in the drawing of a breath." Since then, celluloid and literary vampires have met increasingly spectacular ends, contorting in agony, having their flesh wither and peel from their bones and the bones then turning to dust, or bursting into flames.

Nonetheless, Manchester has gone one step further in his second revised edition of *The Highgate Vampire* (1991), publishing photos said to be time-elapsed exposures of the vampire's final moments.

Regardless of whether one accepts Manchester's account of the Highgate vampire, the case ultimately remains inconclusive. The primary evidence is anecdotal. Reports of mysterious shapes, figures, and noises may have been genuine, but they must be considered in light of possible natural explanations, and of the expectations that many people have that they will encounter something supernatural and frightening in a cemetery. In addition, reports often spawn "me, too" reports, and that seems to have happened in the Highgate case. The case is further clouded by the film production that occurred there during a time of sightings, by possible activities of occult groups, by the extensive media coverage, and by the antics of David Farrant.

The case of the Highgate vampire may never be

proven, but it does stand as one of the most significant modern examples of the power possessed by the vampire image—a power to create a mass horror at the very idea that such a creature could exist. Our fear may be in truth a revulsion at our own collective dark side.

Chapter Six

Strange Encounters

EVERY NOW AND THEN, THE BOUNDARY DIVIDING ORDInary reality from various alternative realities disappears and an individual comes face to face with the unknown. The experience may be an encounter with mysterious beings or forces, such as ghosts, demons, angels, monsters, fairies—and vampires. In the aftermath of such an encounter, the individual may be in awe, excited, puzzled, mystified, frightened—or downright terrified.

Excursions into Vampire Reality take many forms. This chapter takes a look at different ways a vampire or vampire force is reported to have manifested. We'll begin with the classic case of the Vampire of Croglin Grange, an English folktale that stands as one of the vampire encounters closest to the images portrayed in fiction and film—a resurrected corpse said to have left its grave at night to stalk the living.

The Vampire of Croglin Grange

The story of the Croglin Grange vampire is set in Cumberland (now part of Cumbria), England, during the Victorian days. A vivid account of the incident was recorded by Dr. Augustus Hare, a stalwart clergyman of good repute who lived in a rectory in Devonshire, in his autobiographical book *Memorials of a Quiet Life* (1871).

Hare, an author of numerous European guidebooks, was not one to embroider facts with fancy in order to create a juicy tale. He was a matter-of-fact fellow, and had had at least one encounter with a ghost himself, which he dealt with in a most straightforward, no-nonsense manner. Shortly after being installed at his rectory, he entered his study one day to find an old woman seated in the armchair by the fire. The woman appeared to be real, but Hare knew that was impossible—there was no such woman in or near the rectory. He shrugged, chalked it up to indigestion, and sat down on her in the chair. She promptly vanished. The next day, he encountered her again in a passage, and boldly rushed up against her. Again she vanished.

After a third encounter, Hare had to find out who this mysterious woman was. He wrote to his sister and asked her to check with two spinsters who were sisters of the clergyman who had preceded him at the rectory. Upon hearing about Hare's encounters, the spinsters were distressed. The ghost was their mother, they said, and she had appeared to them frequently during their stay at the rectory. They had hoped that upon their departure, the old lady would be at rest. Apparently not.

Hare took other family ghosts he heard about in stride. Thus, when a man named Captain Fisher related to him the chilling story of the Croglin Grange vampire, Hare recorded it as it was told. The story he heard may already have been expanded for the benefit of entertainment, but as a folktale, it is believed to have had some basis in fact. This is Hare's rendition of the story:

Fisher may sound a very plebeian name, but this family is of very ancient lineage, and for many hundreds of years they have possessed a very curious place in Cumberland, which bears the weird name of Croglin Grange. The great characteristic of the house is that never at any period of its very long existence has it been more than one story high, but it has a terrace from which large grounds sweep away towards the church in the hollow, and a fine distant view.

When, in lapse of years, the Fishers outgrew Croglin Grange in family and fortune, they were wise enough not to destroy the long-standing characteristic of the place by adding another story to the house, but they went away to the south, to reside at Thorncombe near Guildford, and they let Croglin Grange.

They were extremely fortunate in their tenants, two brothers and a sister. They heard their praises from all quarters. To their poorer neighbours they were all that is most kind and beneficent, and their neighbours of a higher class spoke of them as a most welcome addition to the little society of the neighbourhood. On their parts, the tenants were greatly delighted with their new residence. The arrangement of the house, which would have been a trial to many, was not so to them. In every respect Croglin Grange was exactly suited to them.

The winter was spent most happily by the new inmates of Croglin Grange, who shared in all the little social pleasures of the district, and made themselves very popular. In the following summer, there was one day which was dreadfully, annihilatingly hot. The brothers lay under the trees with their books, for it was too hot for any active occupation. The sister sat in the verandah and worked, or tried to work, for, in the intense sultriness of that summer day, work was next to impossible. They dined early, and after dinner they still sat out in the verandah, enjoying the cool air which came with evening; and they watched the sun set, and the moon rise over the belt of trees which separated the grounds from the churchyard, seeing it mount the heavens till the whole lawn was bathed in silver light, across which the long shadows from the shrubbery fell as if embossed, so vivid and distinct were they.

When they separated for the night, all retiring to their rooms on the ground-floor (for, as I said, there was no upstairs in that house), the sister felt that the heat was still so great that she could not sleep, and having fastened her window, she did not close the shutters—in that very quiet place it was not necessary—and, propped against the pillows, she still watched the wonderful, the marvellous beauty of that summer night. Gradually she became aware of two lights, two lights which flickered in and out in the belt of trees which separated the lawn from the churchyard, and as her gaze became fixed upon them, she saw them emerge, fixed in a dark substance, a definite ghastly *something*, which seemed every moment to become nearer, increasing in size and substance as it approached. Every now and then it was lost for a moment in the long shadows which stretched across the lawn from the trees, and then it emerged larger than ever, and still coming on—on. As she watched it, the most uncontrollable horror seized her. She longed to get away, but the door was close to the window and the door was locked on the inside, and while she was unlocking it she must be for an instant nearer to *it*. She longed to scream, but her voice seemed paralysed, her tongue glued to the roof of her mouth.

Suddenly—she could never explain why afterwards—the terrible object seemed to turn to one side, seemed to be going round the house, not to be coming to her at all, and immediately she jumped out of bed and rushed to the door, but as she was unlocking it she heard scratch, scratch, scratch upon the window, and saw a hideous brown face with flaming eyes glaring in at her. She rushed back to the bed, but the creature continued to scratch, scratch, scratch upon the window. She felt a sort of mental comfort in the knowledge that the window was securely fastened on the inside. Suddenly the scratching sound ceased, and a kind of pecking sound took its place. Then, in her agony, she became aware that the creature was unpicking the lead! The noise continued, and a diamond pane of glass fell into the room. Then a long bony finger of the creature came in and turned the handle of the window, and the window opened, and the creature came in; and it came across the room, and her terror was so great that she could not scream, and it came up to the bed, and it twisted its long, bony fingers into her hair, and it dragged her head over the side of the bed and—it bit her violently in the throat.

As it bit her, her voice was released, and she screamed with all her might and main. Her brothers rushed out of their rooms, but the door was locked on the inside. A moment was lost while they got a poker and broke it open. Then the creature had already escaped through the window, and the sister, bleeding violently from a wound in the throat, was lying unconscious over the side of the bed. One brother pursued the creature, which fled before him through the moonlight with gigantic strides, and eventually seemed to disappear over the wall into the churchyard. Then he rejoined his brother by his sister's bedside. She was dreadfully hurt, and her wound was a very definite one, but she was of strong disposition, not either given to romance or superstition, and when she came to herself she said, "What has happened is most extraordinary and I am very much hurt. It seems inexplicable, but of course there *is* an explanation, and we must wait for it. It will turn out that a lunatic has escaped from some asylum and found his way here." The wound healed, but the doctor who was sent to her would not believe she could bear so terrible a shock so easily, and insisted that she must have change, mental and physical; so her brothers took her to Switzerland.

Being a sensible girl, when she went abroad, she threw

141

herself at once into the interests of the country she was in. She dried plants, she made sketches, she went up mountains, and, as autumn came on, she was the person who urged that they should return to Croglin Grange. "We have taken it," she said, "for seven years, and we have only been there one; and we shall always find it difficult to let a house which is only one story high, so we had better return there; lunatics do not escape every day." As she urged it, her brothers wished nothing better, and the family returned to Cumberland. From there being no upstairs in the house, it was impossible to make any great change in their arrangements. The sister occupied the same room, but it is unnecessary to say she always closed her shutters, which, however, as in many old houses, always left one top pane of the window uncovered. The brothers moved, and occupied a room together exactly opposite that of their sister, and they always kept loaded pistols in their room.

The winter passed most peacefully and happily. In the following March, the sister was suddenly awakened by a sound she remembered only too well—scratch, scratch, scratch upon the window, and, looking up, she saw, climbed to the topmost pane of the window, the same hideous brown shrivelled face, with glaring eyes, looking in at her. This time she screamed as loud as she could. Her brothers rushed out of their room with pistols, and out the front door. The creature was already scudding away across the lawn. One of the brothers fired and hit it in the leg, but still with the other leg it continued to make way, scrambled over the wall into the churchyard, and seemed to disappear into a vault which belonged to a family long extinct.

The next day the brothers summoned all the tenants of Croglin Grange, and in their presence the vault was opened. A horrible scene revealed itself. The vault was full of coffins; they had been broken open, and their contents, horribly mangled and distorted, were scattered over the floor. One coffin alone remained intact. Of that the lid had been lifted, but still lay loose upon the coffin. They raised it, and there, brown, withered, shrivelled, mummified, but quite entire, was the same hideous figure which had looked in at the windows of Croglin Grange, with the marks of a recent pistol-shot in the leg; and they did the only thing that can lay a vampire—they burnt it.

The story ends here; we can assume that the sister suffered no ill effects and was not troubled again.

The tale of the "old vampire" remains alive in modern-day Cumbria. Croglin Low Hall, a farm south of the Scottish border near Corby Castle, still exists, part of an ancient countryside that was settled long before the Romans arrived in Britain. A tree-lined drive leads to an arch or gateway that opens on a yard surrounded on three sides by farm buildings. A white door, decorated with several horseshoes—amulets to protect against evil spirits—leads to the dwelling section of the complex. There, a bricked-up window still marks where the vampire is supposed to have entered the victim's bedroom. The churchyard is about one mile away. Critics have pointed out that the churchyard has no tomb as described in the story; the tomb may have been an embellishment added in the telling and retelling.

The Croglin Grange vampire stands as a classic "vampire encounter": the damsel in distress violently attacked by a repulsive supernatural creature intent upon draining her blood. The finding of the wound upon the corpse, inflicted by the bullet, is a motif that appears in other stories about the returning dead and werewolves as well. The wound is always the telltale sign that identifies the corpse of the walking dead, or the human being who in secret is a werewolf.

Vampire Visitations at Thornton Heath

Not quite as dramatic as the Croglin Grange story, but with an interesting psychological twist, is the Thornton Heath case. In England, bizarre poltergeist phenomena began occurring in the Forbes household at Thornton Heath in 1938. The activity began abruptly and without apparent cause. Objects flew about the house, dropped from ceilings, and materialized from thin air. Glasses shattered. Pungent smells of violets and rotting flesh permeated the air. The focal point of these activities seemed to be the wife, Pat Forbes. The phenomena escalated in frequency and strangeness until Mrs. Forbes reported the horror of being visited and attacked by an invisible vampire at night.

The case attracted the attention of the media, which resulted in a lengthy investigation by Nandor Fodor, a Hungarian lawyer and journalist turned psychical researcher and, later, psychologist. Fodor's theories about psychological causes of some outbreaks of poltergeist activity were ahead of his time. In particular, his theory of the causes of Mrs. Forbes's experiences, including her encounters with a vampire, was so novel at the time that it was rejected by the psychical research establishment, and Fodor was so roundly criticized that he was moved to sue one publication for libel. He chronicled the case in his book *On the Trail of the Poltergeist* (1958).

The disturbances at Thornton Heath, the home of the Forbes family, began on February 19, 1938. Fodor was on the scene by February 24, and his investigation lasted several months. During that time, Mrs. Forbes emerged as a medium who seemed capable of producing apports, or objects materialized out of the air supposedly with the help of spirits. She also said she had the ability to travel out-of-body and visit people at distant locations. She claimed to have more than one control, entities who claim to be the spirits of the dead who communicate through a medium. Mrs. Forbes also seemed to suffer a great deal of emotional and physical trauma during this time, showing burns, welts, and marks upon her body that seemed to appear without physical cause, and enormous swelling of tissues for no apparent reason. On several occasions, she said she felt she was attacked by a spirit tiger, which raked her flesh and left long red claw marks.

The vampire came to visit her on the night of May 18, 1938.

On the morning of May 19, Fodor telephoned Mrs. Forbes and found her so shaken that she said she feared she was going mad. She was, wrote Fodor, suffering from "sheer horror," and was unable to speak to her husband, George, about what had happened to her during the night. Her experience, said Fodor, "read like a page from Bram Stoker's *Dracula*," but nonetheless seemed excruciatingly real and terrifying. He said:

> She awoke feeling something like a human body lying beside her on top of the cover; something cold and hard which she took to be a head was touching her neck. She was unable to move. After a few seconds the thing left her with a flapping of bird's wings. Then she must have fallen asleep, and in the morning she awoke limp and bloodless. She pricked herself and drew no blood. There were two punctures with clots of blood on her neck.

With a Dr. Wills, Fodor examined Mrs. Forbes's neck. They found two irregular and fairly deep punctures behind the sternal mastoid muscle, about one-eighth inch apart. The skin was red and swollen and showed scratch marks around the punctures.

According to Mrs. Forbes's own account, she'd retired the previous night at about 10:15 PM. As she reached the right-hand side of the bed, she heard the fluttering of a bird and noticed that the air was disturbed and vibrating. It occurred to her that a "thing" was present and that it might come again. After her husband came to bed, she fell into a heavy, unnatural sleep, as though knocked out by chloroform. She reported:

> It may have been around midnight that I woke with the sensation that there was something ghastly on my left-hand side (which is away from my husband), on top of the cover. It felt like a human body. Pressing against my neck was something cold and hard, about the size of a man's head. I could not move, I could not shout, I was frozen with fear. I felt myself getting weaker and weaker, sinking. I felt like this when I lost a lot of blood after an operation.

Asked to elaborate, Mrs. Forbes said that as she started to feel weak, she felt the "thing" pressing into her neck. She had the impression of something biting her, but could not distinctly feel lips or teeth. The body of the "thing" lay still, like a dead weight, and felt "cold and nasty," she said. There was no pain, only a tingling sensation in her neck like the pins-and-needles sensation felt when circulation has been cut off to an extremity. A smell of rotten meat permeated the air. When Mrs. Forbes recovered from her paralysis and was able to move, the thing left her suddenly, swishing through the air with a flapping noise like beating wings as it headed toward the window.

Upon awakening, Mrs. Forbes tasted blood in her mouth and noticed her neck was sore. She felt her neck and discovered the two little lumps. There was no blood on her pillow. She felt extremely cold, and her hands and face looked deathly white to her. Even a neighbor noticed her paleness.

Mrs. Forbes also recalled that three weeks earlier, she had had a nightmare about being bitten on the neck, and in the morning had found tiny red marks upon it.

On May 20, Mrs. Forbes went into trance and Fodor asked one of her spirit controls, "Bremba," for an explanation of the bites. Bremba replied that Mrs. Forbes's soul had been cast out of her body, which was now possessed by the spirit of a young Indian girl. Mrs. Forbes's soul was returning in the form of a bird to take its sustenance from her body's blood in order to survive. If the bird was killed, Bremba said, the Indian girl would be forced to leave Mrs. Forbes's body, and her own soul could return.

Later, Mrs. Forbes told Fodor that she had an unaccountable desire to bite her husband on the neck, and did so.

Toward the end of his investigation, Fodor concluded that most, but not all, of the phenomena manifested in the Forbes house had natural explanations and were caused by psychological conditions within Mrs. Forbes. The spirit controls were secondary personalities, and most of the apports were staged by Mrs. Forbes. Fodor believed the "vampire attack" was a fantasy carried to its extreme by self-mutilation. He said Mrs. Forbes had subconsciously caused other physical trauma to herself, including the scratches and burns.

The psychological causes of these phenomena stretched back deep into Mrs. Forbes's childhood. Fodor peeled back layer after layer of her past. She had suffered a great deal of traumatic childhood illness, and had had frightening hallucinatory experiences and visions of ghosts. Her childhood home seemed to be haunted by a ghost who cleaned the windows and polished the mirrors whenever they became the tiniest bit smudged. By her teen years, she had a strong desire to run away from everything, and by age seventeen had run off to get married against her father's wishes. Her second child died in infancy—another severe shock—and in her twenties she suffered from hysterical blindness, coma, a debilitating kidney ailment, cancer of the breast, and alienation from her husband. She expressed a bizarre attraction to graveyards.

While all of these things were contributing factors, the key factor remained missing. At last, in a free association test, in which Mrs. Forbes responded to words given by Fodor with the first thoughts that entered her mind, repressed memories of a childhood rape in the woods surfaced.

Fodor theorized that as a child, Mrs. Forbes suppressed the horror of the rape by "cutting off" a part of herself—part of her was dead. She had essentially experienced a sort of psychic lobotomy, in which part of the mental system was torn off and left free-floating like a disembodied entity, but capable of personality development on its own. The window- and mirror-polishing ghost was the first manifestation of Mrs. Forbes's pent-up psychic energies. The energies were stirred again on her wedding night, which brought the rape horror closer to the surface of her consciousness and resulted in an unconscious desire to retaliate against her husband for what Fodor termed "the burdens of her soul." To retaliate, she turned on herself.

Fodor unfortunately was not allowed to conclude his investigation and see Mrs. Forbes to a resolution. His tracing of psychic phenomena to a sexual neurosis outraged the Council of the International Institute for Psychical Research, under whose auspices he was working. In the ensuing storm of controversy, Fodor was dismissed from his post as research officer for the institute, and the institute's chairman, J. Arthur Findlay, resigned in protest over Fodor's conclusions on the case. Fodor sued a Spiritualist newspaper for libel, and won two of his four claims in 1939. He then moved to New York, where he became a successful psychoanalyst. Some twenty years later, he still held that his conclusions about the Thornton Heath case were valid. The case has become one of the classics in psychical research, and psychological factors are now routinely considered in similar cases of apparent paranormal phenomena.

The vampire attacks on Mrs. Forbes bear strong resemblance to other cases of similar phenomena that have been documented over centuries, and which are attributed to "biting poltergeists." Such cases are uncommon. Victims are plagued by assailants whose presences may be felt but not seen. They feel bitten, beaten, pinched and scratched. Bite marks and scratches appear on their flesh, raising ugly weals. One case involving a German man, dating to about the early seventeenth century, resembles both the Croglin

Grange and the Thornton Heath cases. A biting assailant plagued him for six years, repeatedly smashing every window pane in his study, and leaving impressions of teeth marks on his skin, including two big fangs that were "sharp as pins."

These occurrences are attributed to psychological conditions, witchcraft, demons and the Devil, depending on the era and culture in which they occur. They also can be called a type of vampire attack because of the nature of the assault.

The Irish "Guardian Vampire"

Grace [not her real name], a modern American woman, has lived with a secret for years: She has a ghostly female vampire companion who visits her at night and talks to her. Unlike the traditional vampire who comes in search of blood, Grace's vampire comes to transfuse Grace with energy. One day in 1990, Grace decided to share her secret with someone who might be understanding. She picked up the telephone and called Jeanne Youngson, founder and president of the Count Dracula Fan Club in New York City.

Youngson, always with a sympathetic, nonjudgmental ear for her callers, took down Grace's story. As is often the case with Youngson's callers, the act of sharing secrets relieves a burden and is an end unto itself. So it was with Grace. She declined to meet Youngson or me in person.

On the telephone, Youngson probed Grace's background and her interest in vampire films and literature. Youngson has found that the answers to such questions sometimes provide clues that help explain a person's experience.

"Grace says that she had the normal exposure to vampire fiction and film, but was never much interested in either," Youngson told me following Grace's phone call. "She never had any other unusual encounters or experiences with ghosts or spirits, nor has she ever been haunted. She is not particularly psychic, but has had a few times when she knew when someone was going to call or write her a letter. Grace jokes about the shortage of men, but seems content with the life she is now leading. She is the head of her department at a company in New Jersey, and she told me that she has started taking voice lessons to get rid of her New England accent. She doesn't make any effort to fix herself up, and is rather plain but very pleasant in appearance. Her most striking feature is her beautiful red hair, which she wears long."

This is Grace's story, as recorded by Youngson:

I came from a big family. I had several older brothers and I was the youngest. I was a mistake and my father never let me or Mother forget it. My mother looked haggard and worn, and she was, from overwork. She had come from Ireland and met my father in church. He came from a large Italian family. My mother's folks had died and she had a distant relative in Connecticut. She worked as a domestic in Ireland until she saved enough money to get to the United States. She always cried when she talked about Ireland, which annoyed my father. He thought Italy was the greatest place in the world, although he never made any attempt to visit there. He called her feeling for Ireland "sentimental drivel."

My brothers were all either very bright or stupid. The two oldest became lawyers, and the others were blue-collar workers. They either had no ambition or just couldn't hack it. My father was a laborer, and although he thought he was a smart guy, it was my mother who really had the brains in the family.

My father was always putting me and Mother down. He thought women were actually inferior to men.

I got excellent grades in school, but Dad said I probably sucked up to the teachers or cheated on my exams. I wanted to go to college and applied to Bridgeport, but when he found out, he made an appointment for me at the phone company and I ended up working there instead of going on to college. We all had to mind our father, or we'd get whipped with his belt. Sometimes he'd knock us down and kick us, but that only happened a few times. He really hurt Tony, one of my brothers, one time, and I think it scared him a bit.

I promised Mom I would go to Ireland as soon as I could, and she started a little nest egg for my trip out of her household money. Only the two of us knew where the "bank" was hidden.

When I was twenty-one she had a stroke and died after two weeks in the hospital. I was delegated to quit my job and stay at home, but I finally rebelled. I told my father I was leaving home. He was livid, but couldn't do anything about it. He had, for years, accused me of being a whore, which was funny since I had very few dates. He locked me out more than once when I'd gone to the movies with a girlfriend, and I had to go spend the night with Grandmother, his mother, next door. He really seemed crazy sometimes, but Grandmother said he was just overworked, supporting the family. I was farsighted and had to wear glasses that made my eyes look enormous, but I had attractive frames and people were always complimenting me on my beautiful, thick red hair, which I had inherited from Mother.

After I left home, I shared an apartment with one of my co-workers, my supervisor, in fact. She had the biggest room and my bedroom was just a tiny closet affair. She was a fair person, and made me pay only one-quarter of the rent. That gave me an opportunity to continue saving up for my trip to Ireland.

A year later, thanks to Mother's nest egg and my savings, I was ready. I took Aer Lingus and got into Dublin airport in the midmorning. I changed some money and took the bus into the city. I got off at the bus station and went in the direction everyone else was going. I came to a river that seemed to have the city on both sides, and I stood on one of the bridges. It was exciting for many reasons, mostly because of Mother, but also I had never been farther away from home than Boston. I wasn't at all nervous being in a strange place.

I hadn't made any hotel reservations, so I walked up to the main street, O'Connell Street, and went into a hotel and asked the price. It was too rich for my blood, so I walked across the street to another place that didn't look so ritzy. The price there was more like it, so I registered and went to my room. I was so excited that I couldn't sleep, so I went out and walked around the streets, Mother's voice ringing in my ears as I looked at the people going on about their business. I wandered into a shopping center in the middle of the city and had something to eat, and then I went out and walked around some more.

I eventually got very tired, but it was only about five in the afternoon. I went into a church and sat until it was dark out. Then I went back to a McDonald's on O'Connell Street and had a hamburger and coffee.

When I got back to my room, I was so wide awake that I didn't think I'd ever get to sleep. There was no TV, so I settled down in my bed and listened to my little transistor radio. The only station I could get clearly was playing western music. It seemed very strange to be listening to cowboy songs in Ireland, but I later learned that the Irish love that kind of music very much.

I guess I dozed off, because I remember waking up and feeling the presence of someone in the room. I put on my glasses and saw a sort of person in the chair near the window. It was sort of filmy, although I couldn't see through it. There was a silhouette of a person, but no features, if you know what I mean. I knew it was a woman, there was just something womanish about the form. The way she was dressed reminded me of someone in an antique wedding gown. I never felt for a second that it was a man.

This person started talking to me in an old-lady kind of voice, and she talked for a long time. She told me she had been born in 1581 and that she only appeared to special people. She said she knew I was unhappy, but that I would be happy again. She told me she was a vampire, but for me not to be frightened, as she had no intention of harming me, but was going to help me. I fell asleep while she was still talking, and when I woke up the sun was shining and I felt *great*.

She appeared in my room every night after that while I was in Ireland, and when I flew back, she came, too.

After a few weeks I felt really strong, and decided to leave Connecticut, so I transferred to a company in New Jersey. It wasn't long before I got a raise and I put a down payment on a house there. I even bought a secondhand car so I could commute.

About my vampire—her name is Mary O'Dwyre. I think she takes energy from other people and somehow gives it to me. I never know when she is going to show up, but it is always at night just before I go to sleep, especially when I am very tired.

She has told me many times that she is over 400 years old, and her voice is like a very old woman's. I can't make out her features. She always sits on the other side of the room, near a window, and she always seems to have the same light-colored filmy outfit on.

I believe she exists in her own way, and that she may be an ancestor of my mother's. I am always glad to see her, because I know I am going to feel good the next day. I don't think she is evil, and of course I have never told any of my co-workers about her. I think of her as being my "guardian vampire," and she doesn't interfere with my work or my social life. I've more or less given up my family in New Haven. I'm not interested in my brothers' wives or children, and I am still resentful of my father for being so mean to me. I guess he didn't know any better. He was a stupid man, I see that now, but his behavior left scars on me and I think he was one of the reasons why my mother died so young.

Brother, Can You Spare a Pint?

Dan [a pseudonym] works the graveyard shift as medical technologist in a hospital in Ohio. One night around Christmas 1989, Dan had an eerie and unsettling experience. This is what he told me:

I was working in the hospital blood transfusion department. I work with my back to the door, but this night I had the uncanny feeling that someone was watching me. I turned and saw a well-dressed man standing just outside the door. He was slight of build and slightly taller than me—I stand six feet. He had on a dark suit, but I can't remember if it was black. His hair was dark.

I asked him if I could help him. He said yes. I asked him what he needed. He said he needed some blood. I asked if he had a blood pickup slip. He said no. I asked if he was a doctor and he said he was, but he never gave me a name. He really made me uneasy, and he wasn't any doctor that I knew. Besides, it was rare for a doctor to pick up blood. He didn't seem interested in talking, anyhow. He was silent and only spoke when I put forward questions. His attention was directed to the cooler full of units of blood behind me.

He then asked if he could come in. I told him he couldn't. I called security because I figured he was either a patient wandering around or else he was a family member of someone who was hospitalized. He stayed at the door until security came. That was the last of it, or so I thought.

About twenty minutes later I felt that the presence was back. Turning toward the door, I saw the same man. He said that he needed blood. Instead of messing with him further, I called security right away. He stayed put until security once again came to remove him. They swore that they had made him leave the hospital after I talked to him the first time. At night, the only way into the hospital is through the emergency room entrance, but nevertheless he managed to slip back in and come back up to the lab. Security said they had no idea how he had gotten back in.

The rest of the night passed without incident.

Dan told a co-worker about the strange visitor determined to get blood. The co-worker, an occult enthusiast, suggested immediately that the man was a blood-starved vampire who was forced to wait for the traditional invitation to come in. Dan found it hard to believe that he had encountered one of the true Undead—a satanist was a more likely explanation, he said. The mysterious, dark-haired man never returned, but Dan still recalls the sharp unease his presence brought.

Maurice Schwalm and the Stull Cemetery Vampire Ghost

Stull, Kansas, is a tiny stop on a long stretch of County Road 442, about ten miles east of Topeka. It boasts a gas station, a store, and a church, and if you're not in need of any of those, you just keep on driving. Settled in the mid-1800s by German immigrants, Stull reached its peak population of about fifty during the first half of the twentieth century. Current residents number about twenty. Stull's claims to fame today are its cemetery and an abandoned, ruined limestone church that sits on Emmanuel Hill, overlooking the graveyard. The cemetery has long been said to be haunted, and the abandoned church is reputedly the site of visits by the Devil. Maurice Schwalm, an investigator of hauntings who lives in Kansas City, Missouri, has a theory that the focal point of the cemetery's hauntings is a vampire ghost attached to a certain grave. His theory is based upon an apparent encounter with this entity.

Vampire ghosts, as distinct from vampires, exist in

the lore of several European countries and India. Invisible, they roam about making strange gibbering noises, and sometimes attack human beings, leaving bite marks on the skin.

Stull—originally named Deer Creek Settlement— is steeped in supernatural lore. According to legend, the early settlers practiced witchcraft, and at least one witch was said to have been hanged from a tree in the graveyard. Later, the settlers wished to repent their ways, and so built the Emmanuel Church in 1867 atop the hill. Another legend holds that the cemetery is haunted because a stableboy killed the town's mayor there in the 1850s. There is no historical basis for these legends, although the German immigrants did bring their witchcraft practices and superstitions with them from the Old World. The curses and cures of the *hexenmeisters* caused some early ministers to write that the place had no respect for the Sabbath. As for the stableboy legend, the cemetery wasn't plotted until the church was built in 1867, and the town never had a mayor. Nonetheless, people say something peculiar exists in Stull.

The old limestone church was closed in the early 1900s after a new church was built down the hill. All that's left of the old church today is a shell—half the roof, the windows, the door, and the wooden floor are missing. Trees grow inside. The cemetery below is still active; that is, burials are still made there.

For several decades, Stull has fascinated University of Kansas students from nearby Lawrence and the curious. Hundreds converge on the place in a frenzy at the "Quarter Days," the times when the Devil suppos- edly appears and wields his dark power. The greatest crowds gather at Halloween and Easter. Devil worshipers are said to frequent the ruined Emmanuel Church, where they perform their blood rites and leave behind occult graffiti and the mutilated remains of sacrificed small animals. Locals complain about vandalism to the headstones in the cemetery, which have been defaced, broken, and even ripped out of their anchors and dragged about. The locals blame the college kids, but some other force may be afoot.

"Some of those headstones are hunks of marble that weigh hundreds of pounds and are attached to flat plates with steel reinforcing rods," said Schwalm. "If the major damage is done by kids, they must be using pickup trucks with winches or cables. It's hard for me to imagine how they could accomplish that in the middle of the night."

Many of the curious who visit the locale at night in search of a supernatural thrill get more than they bargained for. They see hallucinations of ghostly human beings standing in the road, bleeding church walls, burning crosses, and red glows around the abandoned church. With tape recorders, they capture disembodied voices whispering in the night. Some fall to the ground in convulsions, and others experience mysterious time-lapse blackouts. Runs of bad luck, accidents, and disasters curse some long after they leave.

The college students have added stories of their own to the old legends. They say that a witch child sired by the Devil is buried in the cemetery, and its ghost walks about at night. The name Stull used to be "Skull," they say, a reference to the Devil.

The occult activity at Stull piqued Schwalm's interest, and he set out to investigate the place in 1986. Whenever Schwalm investigates a haunting, he takes photographs first to see if something unusual and inexplicable turns up on the film—an aura, a mist, a cloud, a shape hidden in the background. Spirit photography—the capturing of nonphysical beings or "extras" on film—is a fascinating, but controversial field. It began accidentally in 1861, when a Boston jewelry engraver named William Mumler took a self-portrait and the image of a dead person appeared next to his. At the time, Spiritualism was growing in popularity, and Mumler's discovery touched off a rage for spirit photographs. Many were faked. Spirit photography continues to have its serious students, who, like Schwalm, photograph supernaturally active sites to see what, if anything, manifests.

"I've taken photos of haunted sites for decades and I'm not sure that I've ever seen anything that has showed up on film," said Schwalm, who has conducted more than fifty investigations of hauntings. "A lot of times photography is just trial and error, but sometimes it gives me a little clue as to what is going on.

"I do not consider myself psychic with a capital *p*," he went on. "But where psychic phenomena are concerned, I can see lightning and hear thunder. Something comes through." In the case of Stull Cemetery, "something" did manifest.

Schwalm made his first visit to Stull on March 23, 1986. In the daylight, he took a number of random photographs around the cemetery. When the film was developed, he observed a golden glow around one of the old markers. Believing that he might have found the focal point of the cemetery's haunting, Schwalm began to research the history of the occupant of the grave. It was a seventeen-year-old boy who had died on October 24, 1895, of typhoid fever. The boy had contracted his fatal illness several months after he was crushed beneath an overturned wagon. The marker itself was plain and unremarkable, and strangely had been overlooked in a census taken by the Daughters of the American Revolution in 1940.

"I went back to Stull on April 25, 1986, and things got more interesting," Schwalm said. "I was walking through the place looking for additional places to photograph. I heard a sound like knocking on wood. At the same time, I was aware of what I would describe as a faint dental pressure on the back of my neck, like teeth pressing on the skin. I was also aware of a faint gibbering sound. I took it as a signal to stand my ground and start taking photos. I wasn't frightened because I just regarded it as a way of translating a psychic input into a sensory form that can be used. I didn't think I was under psychic attack because I get along so well with ghosts.

"One of the photos I took at the spot shows what I would describe as a werewolflike form of a boy standing on a tree limb. He seems to be holding out a mask, which to me has some sort of pagan connotations. By pagan, I mean in the sense of Greco-Roman rituals in which players on stage used masks."

Schwalm showed me the photo. A large tree was prominent, set against a background of surrounding foliage. The werewolf shape was not readily identifiable, but could be discerned from the colorations of the background. A skeptic would say that the shape was nothing more than a random pattern formed by the background. A psychic might say otherwise.

Schwalm explained his theory: "I think I did detect the focal point of the haunting on my first visit. When

I went back, our vampirelike friend was afraid that I might be planning some sort of exorcism. I certainly had no intentions of putting a stake through him, but I don't know what his mental processes might have been. I think I was shown the werewolflike form as an indication of how powerful an influence I was dealing with—a 'don't tread on me' message."

I asked Schwalm if there were any clues why the grave of a farmboy who died such a tragic death would be a ghostly focal point. He said none had been discovered, but given the prevalence of old-world magic and witchcraft practices at the time, it's likely that the suffering boy had been subjected to various attempts at magical cures. Perhaps something went wrong. Or perhaps the accident that injured him and the typhoid fever that followed were due to a curse put upon him by an enemy.

Schwalm's third visit to Stull in March 1987 was uneventful. "I don't intend to go back to Stull," Schwalm said. "I don't feel any need to drive a stake through the heart of the corpse. As far as I'm concerned, the cemetery is *his* territory. Even vampires have rights in my book."

Beckoning the Vampire

If you believe in something strongly enough, sooner or later it will manifest in your life. Even if that something is a vampire. Just ask Christiane Raymond.

Raymond, an artist in her early twenties, lives in Auburn, a small town in northern California. Auburn has a reputation for being an artsy community, but not, Raymond says, for her kind of art, which is

Salvador Dali—esque in style, full of human forms with contorted muscles and pronounced arteries and veins. Raymond works in dry media—pen and ink, pencil, and collage—and pursues her vision despite the fact that she feels ostracized by the locals.

"They don't like anything radical in art," she opined. "If you don't draw wagon trains or little flowers in pots, they don't want anything to do with you."

Her family moved to Auburn from southern California in order to escape the latter's materialism. The move left Raymond longing for the bright lights and the cutting-edge culture of the big cities. Raymond has a vivid imagination, which she acknowledges sometimes carries her away. That and her intense interest in vampires provide escape from the ordinariness of her job in her parents' print shop and what she perceives as the narrow confines of the community. Her sense of isolation is intensified by her feeling that she has always been a loner, someone different from others, especially those her age. She cultivates this sense of apartness with behavior that sets her off from others. As a result, she seems to draw people to her or, more often than not, drain them of their energy and push them away.

She often dresses in black and wears occult jewelry. The black intensifies the paleness of her skin (she stays out of the sun), the red of her hair, and the pools of mystery in her large brown eyes. She once owned a black Supra automobile and hung black bats in it.

"I'm a rebel," she said. "I consider myself odd. And the vampire is definitely an odd character."

Back in the 1960s, Raymond's mother used to set her on her knee and watch "Dark Shadows," a soap

162

opera with a vampire. That may have planted the seed of interest in vampires, but the seed didn't blossom until 1985, when Raymond discovered Anne Rice's novel *The Vampire Lestat* and devoured it in nearly one sitting. "After that, it was anything and everything I could find about vampires," Raymond told me. "Now I think *they* find *me*. The main thing about them that attracts me is the sexual part of it. There's something very sensuous about the act of vampirism, the biting and the sucking of blood. They're very romantic characters. They have immortality—they go on forever and see so many different changes in the world. They're sort of time travelers and I've always thought that would be neat. The character Lestat is the epitome, the ultimate vampire to me.

"The more I read stories about vampires, the more I identified with them," Raymond said. "Lately I've experimented. The other night I cut my finger badly and it started to bleed like crazy. Without thinking about it, I put my mouth over my finger and started to suck the blood out. I didn't think about what I was doing. Finally I stopped and thought, Wow! I'm really doing this. That was exciting. I *was* surprised that the blood didn't have much taste. The closest thing I can compare it to is eating a rare steak that has that irony, earthy taste. Since then, if I cut my finger, I immediately start licking at it. I don't think, Oh, I'm going to suck this because that's what a vampire would do. I just do it.

"At this point, I can't imagine cutting my finger purposely so that I could drink blood. But if somebody were to approach me about getting together to drink blood, I probably would try it and see if it was something I needed.

"I don't rule out the possibility of there being real, honest-to-goodness vampires because it's so perfect for them these days," Raymond explained. "They don't have to go out and get victims. They can go to blood banks. There are people stockpiling blood all the time."

"Have you ever wished you were a vampire?" I asked.

"Yes, all the time. It's gotten progressively worse, as a matter of fact. If given the chance, I definitely would become a vampire. Vampires have the world at their disposal. They live forever and don't have to worry what's going to happen the next day. They're self-sufficient. They don't need a dwelling but can live in a cave or a hole. They're not subject to the trials of mortal life that we all have to go through. Their physical power appeals to me, too, because I'm not a very big person. I'm only about five foot four and weigh about 105 pounds."

"How do you fantasize about being a vampire?"

"I have a bat ring that my sister bought me last November for my birthday. It gets a lot of attention and people ask why I wear it. They freak out when I start telling them. I've always thought how neat it would be if I could fly up to their windows and flap myself on the glass and say, 'Hi, guys, you thought I was joking, didn't you?'

"Shape-shifting appeals to me," Raymond went on. "I love animals, and to become one and run with them would be the ultimate experience. I also love the nighttime. To be able to get around and do my own thing in the night and sleep in the day would be great. I love to sleep. The thought of sleeping in a coffin has always appealed to me for some reason. I think that would be a blast, to crawl into a coffin at night—a nice, black lacquered one. I've thought about getting a coffin, but it's a bit difficult when you live with your parents. There's lots of things decor-wise I would do if I had my own place."

"Do your fantasies include biting people?"

"Yes, but only certain types. I don't think I could bring myself to go after anybody who was physically repulsive to me. I couldn't go up to dirty, drunken winos and drink their blood. Only beautiful people. There's a musician I've been interested in ever since high school. He's not well known here. His features are the perfect example of what I picture a vampire to look like. He's androgynous-looking, in his thirties, very pale with long fingers, very piercing blue eyes. He would be my first victim."

I asked if this intense identification with vampires had brought any real vampires into Raymond's life.

She said, "One of my favorite short stories is about a girl who is so obsessed with vampires and wants a vampire lover so bad that she leaves her window open at night and takes care not to leave any silver about or eat any garlic. Eventually he does come.

"The other night, a strange thing happened. My parents had gone out and I was at home by myself. I was sitting on the couch watching a movie in the den but was thinking in general about vampires in connection with a novel I'd been reading, *A Vampire in Moscow*. From the den, you can see through a doorway and down the hall into the living room. The hall was dark and the living room was lit. I suddenly had the strangest sensation. I could have sworn that I saw somebody walk by that door—a black-clothed figure that looked at me briefly. It was male and average in height. I caught a glimpse of face but didn't register any features. I did a double take. That's never happened before, and it gave me the chills for a while."

Asked for an explanation of this manifestation, Raymond said, "Maybe I projected an image of what I was thinking. Sometimes you can almost make things happen, create a thought-form. Maybe subconsciously I pictured somebody walking across the hall and it seemed to be real. This sort of thing has always interested me and I've been receptive to it. After I got over the chills, I took it in my stride and said, 'I expected this sort of thing to happen eventually.'"

"Was there an energy around this manifestation?" I asked.

"It was almost inviting, like 'come and see who I am.' I'm sort of mad I didn't get up off the couch and see if there was somebody really there."

"Do you think it might be the same wish-fulfillment as the story about the vampire lover?"

"I wish it would be," Raymond said. "They say that if you want it bad enough, it can happen. Lately this feeling has been real strong—I want somebody to come and take me away from this ordinary world. If my vampire lover is out there, I wish he'd show himself. Maybe he did. Maybe he was telling me, 'I am here, how far do you want me to take this?'

"I've never had a boyfriend or too many friends. The whole idea of sex has kind of been repulsive to me. When I think about the act of vampirism, that to me is far more sexual than the act that mortals go through. Now, if somebody came up to me and said, 'I want to bit your neck,' that I could go for."

"Do you dream about vampires?"

"I rarely remember my dreams," Raymond said. "But the other morning I woke up and went into the bathroom. I found a big, hardened lump of blood on my lips, as though I'd bitten them. I don't know how it got there. Maybe I just had a wild dream."

Chapter Seven

Devon and the Vampire Choir

THE OUIJA BOARD IS MARKETED AS A GAME, AND HAS BEEN used by many as a means of divination. On the board are the letters of the alphabet, the words "yes" and "no," and numbers. You place your fingertips on a little plastic pointer that sits on three felt-tipped legs, ask a question, and wait to see if the pointer will move to spell out or indicate an answer.

The modern Ouija—the name is taken from the German and French terms for "yes," *oui* and *ja*—was created in 1892 and has enjoyed steady popularity as a parlor game. Some have used it as a device to try to communicate with spirits and the dead. In concept, the Ouija dates back more than 2,500 years—the ancient Chinese, Greeks, and Romans all used similar means to communicate with spirits and the dead and to divine the future.

The game seems harmless enough. Either nothing happens, or perhaps the pointer moves jerkily from letter to letter, most likely propelled by the subconscious desires of the user. Two or more persons can place their fingertips on the pointer and act in concert.

Many persons who have used the Ouija have a good time. Some even have contacted what appear to be evolved and intelligent entities. For example, one of the classics in modern occult literature is *The Betty Book*, written by Stewart Edward White and based upon the communication between his wife, Betty, and a host of spirits called "the Invisibles." Contact with the spirits began in 1919 when the Whites tried the Ouija as a parlor game. The Invisibles progressed to communicating through Betty in automatic writing and then a sort of trance channeling, in which Betty "set aside" her consciousness and relayed what the Invisibles had to say. The spirits' messages dealt with advice for humankind's spiritual progress. After seventeen years of sessions, the Whites organized and published the book.

Similarly, in the 1960s, Jane Roberts, an upstate New York poet and writer, began using the Ouija with her husband and encountered an entity who became known as Seth. Communication with Seth progressed to automatic writing and then direct channeling, in which Seth used the vocal cords of an entranced Roberts to speak. Seth dictated a number of books outlining his esoteric philosophy, which became bestsellers.

Journalist Ruth Montgomery began her occult exploration with seances and the Ouija in the 1950s; she felt the Ouija enabled her to make contact with her dead father and others. Montgomery also progressed to automatic writing, which she said enabled her to communicate with a host of spirits of the dead, all of whom helped her write a string of best-sellers.

However, critics of the Ouija contend it's not so harmless and may even be dangerous. The user asks a question but has little or no control over what comes through. Some psychologists say that the device enables communication with the subconscious. The user risks dredging up repressed material from the depths of the psyche that he or she is unable to deal with, and thus can suffer an adverse reaction. Some occultists and Christian authorities say the board communicates with external forces and invites possession by evil entities. Users who wish to contact spirits more or less put out an open call to anything that's listening. Typically, critics say, those listening entities are malicious, earthbound spirits whose sole purpose is to amuse themselves by tormenting human beings. If a user is psychically open or psychologically vulnerable, these entities can invade and take over.

Regardless of whether the Ouija reaches in or out, problems with it often follow a pattern. The messages seem to come from a personality who gives a name, and who initially seems friendly, helpful, and amusing. The user, thoroughly entertained and intrigued, spends more and more time at the board, consulting what appears to be an amazing oracle. After the user becomes dependent on the communication, the messages turn darker and harsher. The user then is instructed to do unpleasant or dangerous things, or is threatened with death at the hands of the spirit. The entity may communicate or manifest without being summoned through the board. At that point, extreme measures are required to disengage from the situation. Users may require psychological counseling and therapy. Some turn to religion for help in casting out demons.

In 1970–71 in Connecticut, two sixteen-year-old high school girls took up the Ouija and sent out an open call. What answered claimed to be a vampire.

Devon, as the vampire introduced himself, quickly established a rapport with Ann and Mary [pseudonyms], who were fans of "Dark Shadows." He seemed to be a likable and charming personality. Mary, tall and slender with straight dark hair that fell well below her shoulders, shared the secret about Devon with a third girl whom she knew casually, a fifteen-year-old named Eva [also a pseudonym]. Eva was soon swept into the romantic intrigue with Ann and Mary and their vampire friend.

Eva is now in her thirties and works in financial services in the Southwest. She recalled her experiences for me, but it wasn't easy; for years she had deliberately tried to forget some of the memories in an effort to detach herself from the unpleasant events that unfolded.

The focal point of the intrigue with Devon was Ann, a secretive but charismatic girl with long, light brown hair and an inscrutable face. She was a marvel at the Ouija board. She would take off her glasses and place her fingertips on the pointer. She was so nearsighted that she could not read the letters without her glasses, yet the pointer would zoom around the board so fast that Mary and Eva had trouble keeping up with the messages. Ann undoubtedly was psychically open. Her mother was involved in the occult, and had raised Ann with a host of magical practices and objects. Ann kept a chest in her bedroom that was full of magical objects, including "luckies," or amulets, and wax figurines for casting spells. Ann's mother wasn't directly involved in the communications with the vampire, but perhaps had provided some fertile ground for the wrong kind of unsupervised occult activity.

Devon told the girls that he and Ann had been cousins in past lives in eighteenth-century England. He had been the Earl of Devonshire, he said, and he and Ann were romantically involved. A jealous third party had put a curse on Devon to become a vampire forever. He'd fed on Ann's blood and accidentally killed her by draining too much. Now Devon was able to reunite with his love in her latest incarnation through the Ouija, and he sustained himself once again by drinking her blood at night. According to Ann, Devon would often manifest in her bedroom. They would speak directly to one another, and enjoyed a close relationship. She gave him her blood. Sometimes she went out at night on strange nocturnal trips. It remained a mystery, at least to Eva, where she went and what she did.

Ann said Devon was a man of average height and looks with brown hair—a bit like Barnabas Collins, the vampire on "Dark Shadows." He had canine fangs. But instead of swallowing the blood when he bit, he sucked it up through his fangs, which were hollow like straws.

This peek at the supernatural fascinated Eva. She had been raised a devout Christian, and only the summer before had had a profound religious experience while participating in a missionary program in the Orient. When Mary suggested that Eva spend the night at her house so that the three of them could talk to Devon, Eva eagerly agreed. She wasn't sure why Mary was drawing her into her confidence—Ann was opposed to it—but Eva wanted to go along for the ride, and Ann finally agreed. Perhaps Mary had involved Eva intuitively as a stabilizing influence. Eva had a fresh, shiny persona. With dark blond hair and a sweet face, she was the kind of girl whom others felt comfortable to be around and to confide in. Her grounding in religion may also have appealed to Mary, who may already have sensed a darkening of clouds on the occult horizon.

When the overnight at Mary's came to pass, the girls got out the Ouija and Ann contacted Devon. He entertained them with clever stories and jokes, and elaborated on his past-life history with Ann. Eva had never experienced anything like it.

When the hour grew late, the girls retired. "Ann went to bed first," Eva said. "Mary and I were out of the room when we heard this thumping noise. We walked into her room and turned on the lights in time to see an alarm clock flying through the air toward Ann. It looked like it had been thrown from somewhere on the other side of the room, though there was no one else in the room but her. It fell on her bed. I couldn't believe that this was happening—it was so incredible. To actually see it was very disturbing and horrifying. There was no good explanation for it. It was old hat to Mary and Ann because these things had been going on for some time, but it posed a profound spiritual crisis for me, and I got very upset and started crying. I saw the good spiritual side and the bad spiritual side as mutually exclusive. In traditional Christianity, the only reference to the bad side is to

173

Satan or the Devil. That is handled so abstractly that he has become more a metaphor for evil rather than an entity that can be taken seriously.

"Seeing Devon on the bad side, I thought that the good side was precluded from existing. I'd never heard it discussed that good and bad spiritual entities could operate in the same universe. I don't think that now, of course, but it was my feeling at the time. I'd never heard about this weird stuff in church and nobody had ever told me about it. I could see that the clock flying across the room was real. But I didn't have the same sort of evidence that God was real, so I figured God must be a lie. I kind of gave up on my faith on the spot and became wholeheartedly involved in the occult. It seemed to me that there was much more evidence for that than there was for Christianity.

"Even now, I'm still at a bit of a loss to describe the impact this experience had on me. The only words that come to mind are 'overwhelming' to describe its scope and 'devastating' to describe its effect."

Eva became involved in regular sessions with the Ouija. "Devon talked a lot of his past and present love for Ann," Eva said. "In many ways, his story paralleled 'Dark Shadows' and vampire movies."

Devon also made the girls laugh. "Early on we asked Devon what he did during the day," said Eva. "He said he spent most of his time hanging out in women's dressing rooms in department stores watching them try on clothes. Cheap thrills! We thought it was pretty funny."

The girls kept using the Ouija because, said Eva, "it was such a thrill—you know, esoteric knowledge that we were the only ones privy to. We felt like we were part of the elite who had personal experience of this kind. It was so darn fascinating. The romantic story was appealing. In the teen years you tend to feel so alienated anyway, and this was our own secret thing. It didn't seem dangerous at the time. By the time that we felt we were in danger, it was almost too late to get out of it."

Devon soon introduced the girls to a group of about seven or eight invisible vampire friends. Collectively they called themselves the Choir, though each had his own name. "These beings had marked personalities and seemed like real people," Eva said. "They had their own quirks. They seemed to have a sense of humor and they had fun with us, telling us stories that would appeal to us."

Devon and the Choir boys began leaving gifts at night for the girls. Ann had a "gift bowl" in her room where the presents supposedly would materialize overnight. The next day, she would deliver the items to Eva or Mary, or tell the girls what Devon had left for her. Ann told Eva that one of the Choir, named Jonathan Ferris, was interested in her. Jonathan began communicating with Eva through the Ouija. Jonathan left gifts for Eva in the gift bowl. Once Eva received a book on the French impressionists, given because Jonathan had said they had lived in nineteenth-century France in a relationship parallel to that of Devon and Ann.

The girls were witness to strange physical phenomena that seemed to have no natural explanation. At first, the phenomena were scary. Then the shock would wear off—until something else happened. Devon claimed to wear long fingernails, and the girls could hear the sounds of clicking nails. It had to be

Devon and not any of them—their nails were bitten to the quick. Bedcovers were yanked by invisible hands. Odd tappings and noises sounded, and objects moved around the room in the dark when the girls were together.

"Once I saw direct evidence of vampiric activity when I spent a night at Ann's house," Eva said. "She and I were in twin beds in the same room. She was talking to me in the dark and all of a sudden stopped. I heard this noise that sounded like a can being opened with a can opener, a kind of a popping noise, and then this disgusting slurping noise. I kept calling her name and she wouldn't answer. I was afraid to turn on the light, but I did and saw that she was covered with blood and had holes in her neck. She was semiconscious. She had blood all over her neck and down her nightgown. I was scared to death! I tried to clean her up and stop the blood flowing. I didn't see anything or anybody in the room.

"Later Ann was embarrassed at what had happened. Allegedly this blood-drinking went on quite often, but Mary and I weren't witness to it. Ann was sick and absent from school often, and when she did show up she looked pale and drained. We became afraid she was going to die."

Devon began taking spirit possession of Ann. She would go into a trance and her voice would change, deepening and taking on an English accent as Devon spoke directly to those present.

Ann eventually told Eva and Mary that, according to Devon, the real present-day Ann had died and her body had been taken over permanently by her eighteenth-century self, who had had the same first name.

As part of this transformation, Ann's handwriting became flowery—and remains so to the present day. She also continues to use English word spellings, such as "colour" and "favourite."

Sometimes Devon also would take physical possession of Ann. "Devon would show up at school occasionally, supposedly in Ann's body, because he wanted to see what school was like," Eva said. "In one incident, I was talking to her and said something about algebra, and she said, 'What's algebra?' She gave a bizarre smile and said, 'I'm not Ann.'"

Devon and the Choir also lost their charming veneers. "No more Mr. Nice Guy, no more cute stories," Eva said. The girls began to feel they were losing control over the situation. "I think things were always out of control and it was a delusion to think we had any control," Eva said. "We thought we were so powerful."

In an effort to regain control, Mary convinced Ann and Eva to admit several newcomers to their seance circle—three boys and a girl, all about eighteen years old, who claimed to be practitioners of witchcraft and magic. The seven of them called themselves a coven. Though the girls ostensibly held the power, the boys were very much in control, since they were older and more experienced. The coven studied the raising of psychic power, spell casting, and the use of amulets and talismans. One of the boys was interested in black magic. "He would try the use of power to get things he wanted. He tried to get all of us in bed at times in order to break our power and subjugate us. I tried to transfer energy to him. One time he tried to conjure demons by name. He was a lot more trouble than he was help because he had his own little agenda. There was a lot of drug use by some of the others. They smoked marijuana a lot, and one guy had taken too much mescaline in the past and was kind of spaced-out. He presented himself as a white witch, but a lot of the things he said were farfetched. None of the three of us girls were particular drug users."

After the introduction of magic, the physical phenomena increased. There still seemed to be no natural explanation, as Eva could see the others clearly at the time strange things happened. There would be rappings on the walls that went around the room, each wall in quick succession. Eva and others were tapped on the head by unseen hands. Bits of newspaper were mysteriously crumpled up and thrown at them from nowhere. Bed slats were banged. Ann continued to take on Devon's personality in a frightening way. At one seance, Ann was going under when suddenly a tape recorder on the other side of the room erupted with wild laughter. Finally, Devon and the Choir threatened to kill the girls. "At one point, we all were supposed to die at a certain hour," Eva said. "It was supposed to happen during the day while we were at school. We wandered around aimlessly, wondering what we were going to do. Ironically, all I could think of was that if I was going to die, I didn't have to do my social studies homework. But nothing happened to us. We were quite relieved."

What terrified Eva the most was the beginning of phenomena in her own home when none of the other coven members were present. " 'Greensleeves' was Devon's favorite song. One morning I came downstairs and found the record player was on. The arm was moving back and forth across a record like it was stuck. It was the 'Greensleeves' record. Nobody in my family had put it there. It was like somebody had been listening to it during the night. Another incident involved our bust of Josephine, Napoleon's wife. My mother would come down in the morning and that thing would be turned around to face the wall. She couldn't figure it out. According to Devon, he and the Choir turned it around because it offended them—the English and the French were enemies. That's what blew me away—that *these things were going on in my house when none of the others involved were there.* It was frightening. It wasn't localized anymore and I knew that I was in it over my head, I was an integral part of it, and I couldn't get out of it without trouble. I was afraid I was going to become a focal point like Ann."

At the same time, bats began invading Eva's home. Bats are common in Connecticut, and every now and then one finds its way into the typical home, but Eva's home seemed to be under siege. "My parents couldn't figure out how they were getting into the house," she said. "They stopped up the chimney, they put special screens on the windows, and the bats still got in. We came back from a trip and found one dead in the bathtub. A couple got into the basement. We'd hear them going overhead at night. I had this canopy bed. One night I heard this flapping noise in my room. I turned on the light and saw a dark brown bat, about five inches long, hanging upside down from the canopy. I shrieked. I woke my father up and he came in and took it out.

"Besides the bat problems, I would hear knockings

179

in the attic that sounded like people walking around. It may have been just house noises, but by then I could barely sleep anymore. I would go to bed with a cross and a Bible and amulets and leave the light on. I was terrified. I never said anything at the time to my parents—they had no idea what was really going on. They became concerned about me because I wouldn't sleep in the dark. My mother asked me, 'Why do you sleep with the light on? Do you see things in the dark?' like I was an eight-year-old child. I was unable to offer an explanation. Oh, Mom, if you only knew!"

A way out appeared for Eva when she confided her situation to a Christian friend. "He said it was obvious that we were under attack by demons. That was a bizarre revelation to me, because I thought these were some sort of beings with bodies. I never thought of them as pure spirits or demons."

Eva was told that she was possessed. She agreed to attend a Pentecostal service to have the demons cast out. In all, she subjected herself to three charismatic exorcisms. The first two took place in Connecticut, the third in Minnesota, where she went to attend college.

But the exorcisms proved to be as terrifying as the encounters with the vampires. "I went through some harrowing experiences that just about killed me when I was taken to Pentecostal churches," Eva said. "In one instance, the lights had gone off in the church building. I fainted and they carried me in. I heard myself scream, but it was like I wasn't there. A man was calling out these demon names and it was all dark. The congregation was singing 'in the spirit'—a harmonious but unstructured type of singing. They had their hands all over me. It was a horrible experience.

"In another instance, the minister grabbed my head and shook me real hard and screamed for the demons to come out. I wanted to say, 'Hey, look, *I'm* in here and you're hurting me!' That was a terrible experience. In another case, there was some sort of ceremony where they told me I couldn't leave until I was baptized in the Holy Spirit and spoke in tongues. I flatly refused, to their extreme disappointment. The last thing I wanted to do was lose control of my speech! I was scared of them, and was afraid that if the bad side didn't get me, the Christians would."

I asked Eva if she herself had felt possessed. "To a certain extent," she answered. "There *was* something wrong and out of my control. I had temporary benefit from the exorcisms, but it all came back on me. Exorcism isn't something that can be done to you. You have to connect to the bad and replace it with something good to keep it from recurring. I was able to get rid of it through a relationship with a man I started going out with in college. I made a conscious decision to keep out of any kind of occult activity. I threw away a lot of my clothes, amulets, books, and things that reminded me of what had happened. I made a clean sweep."

While Eva was in college, she experienced one final manifestation that was a vestige of the Ouija vampires. "I was friends with a guy, a former boyfriend, who knew about my history," she said. "He was good friends with someone who wanted to write a book on vampires, whom I'll call Tom. Tom came out to interview me. He was fascinated because he had never heard of an experience like mine. We ended up going out and getting close. He was not able to distance himself from my story and treat it objectively—he thought he could research it without becoming intimately involved, but it was apparent to me that he was obsessed with the occult in general and vampires in particular, and was courting a direct experience himself. Ann visited me once, and when she found out what Tom was trying to do, she called him and tried to dissuade him from becoming involved. Both Ann and I thought he was getting into something that he didn't fully understand.

"While I was still seeing Tom, there was an event. I was living in a one-bedroom apartment with another woman. One night I'd gone to bed and she came into the room. She swore that she saw a man standing over my bed. I screamed in my sleep, but I don't know if I was aware of a figure. My roommate didn't know my history, nor was she interested in the occult. After that, I felt that I had to divorce myself from any kind of occult involvement or research and that it would be better to break up with Tom. I did."

Over time, the terror subsided and Eva began to be free of occult harassment. She maintained contact with Mary and Ann, but the vampires were a taboo subject, especially for Ann. "For Ann and Mary, the whole thing just petered out," said Eva. "They never went through a conversion experience like I did. I've always wished that Ann would talk about it because she holds the key to the whole thing. I'd give anything to know what was *really* going on, but it's a totally closed subject with her—that's how she survives, how she copes. Interestingly, when she turned twenty she became diabetic, and diabetes is not in her family. The doctors couldn't figure out why it happened. I don't know if it had anything to do with what happened to us.

"About three years ago, Ann and her husband moved out here near me. Her husband came first and stayed at my house for about three months while he looked for a job. One night we had a conversation and he asked, 'How much do you know about Ann's old boyfriend, Devon?' My jaw could have hit the floor! I said, 'Devon is not human.' He was stunned. He said that in college Ann had talked about a vampire and someone named Devon, but he didn't want to hear anything about it—he thought she was crazy. She eventually told him that Devon was an older man whom she'd gone out with for a while."

As for the witchcraft practitioners who had joined their seances, ill things seemed to befall them. The boy who took mescaline committed suicide. The black magician has been drifting without purpose. A girl has been missing for fifteen years.

Today, Eva feels comfortable living alone. She has five dogs and sleeps with the lights off. "Talking about this now, it sounds insane," she told me. "I think we really did contact demons who masqueraded as vampires because of our fascination with 'Dark Shadows.' They were bored and wanted to play with our heads. They were funny and friendly at first, then got progressively nastier, especially when we tried to get out. Toward the end, the whole story, even the vampirism, was dropped."

Eva has a theory about why the beings took on vampire form. "Blood is a very powerful symbol in the spiritual world. Certainly blood plays a big part in the Judeo-Christian traditions, first in the sacrifice of animals, then in the death of Christ, and subsequently in the divinely inspired Christian ritual of the Eucharist. Blood represents both the mortality of man and the immortality of God, in Christ. The stealing of the life-force of blood is just about the most horrific image a human mind can create. On the other hand, when I was trying to fend off these beings, nothing—Bibles, amulets, garlic, crosses—had the power to disable them more than calling on the Blood of Christ."

Eva raises an interesting point about blood. Since the dawn of civilization, blood has been revered as a substance of great magical power. It has played an important role in both religious and magical rites everywhere around the world. Blood is identified with the soul and is the vehicle that disperses the vital forces of the cosmos throughout the body in order to sustain life. In occult traditions, to possess the blood of another—even a drop or two—was to possess magical power over them.

Eva struggled to put the vampire experience behind her. "After it was all over, I went through a long period of selective forgetting that enabled me to get on with my life. For quite a while, I felt I couldn't see any movies about things along these lines, and I slept with a night-light on.

"I told my family what had happened in about 1973. My parents went into each room in the house and prayed to try to rid the house of any spirits that might still be hanging around. There were no more manifestations there after I left to go to college.

"I'm a Christian again, but I still have problems

dealing with charismatic churches. I think they have some severe misconceptions. I don't think demons are ready to leap out from behind every bush, or can influence everything that people do. Exorcisms, speaking in tongues—that stuff still gives me the creeps to this day. It was more a quiet personal decision on my part that ended it, not some bombastic Pentecostal brouhaha. I don't feel I'm in any danger from this kind of thing anymore. But I've never used the Ouija since, nor would I ever again."

Did Eva and her friends truly contact vampire demons, or were the vampires merely projections from the subconscious of one or all of the girls? Both theories would have their supporters. It also is plausible that both theories might be true in part; Eva agrees this is possible.

The phenomena that occurred—rappings, movements of objects, the alleged paranormal appearance of objects, physical assaults, and equipment suddenly switched on—are characteristic of poltergeist attacks. As we saw in Chapter Six concerning the Thornton Heath vampire case, poltergeist attacks often are attributed to spirits, but can also arise from the right mix of psychological conditions. Much research into poltergeists has been done in recent decades, yet little is known for certain, and the theories remain controversial. Researchers who have pursued Nandor Fodor's theory of repressed neurosis as a cause have found ample supporting evidence. In such cases, real physical phenomena apparently occur as a result of projection of internal energies.

Interestingly, the focal point in many cases is a

female who is under the age of twenty—as was Ann. The teen years are filled with psychological turmoil: alienation, blossoming and repressed sexuality, hostility, problems with self-esteem. In poltergeist cases, these tensions and repressions are thought to boil over unconsciously in acts of psychokinesis (PK), a form of psychic energy that causes physical phenomena to happen. Add the PK tendency to a vivid imagination, a desire to be swept away in a romantic fantasy, and an interest in vampires, and the stage is set for contact with an unseen vampire who becomes progressively real.

That doesn't necessarily mean that Ann deliberately and consciously made up Devon and the Choir. The Ouija could have reached into her subconscious for material that seemed to her and the others to come from an external voice. From there, a number of these other factors could have come into collective play.

In addition, Mary and Eva could have contributed to the phenomena. A parallel might be found in the interesting case of an artificially created poltergeist named Philip. In the early 1970s, eight members of the Toronto Society for Psychical Research set out to try to fabricate a poltergeist personality through collective concentration. First they made up his name, Philip Aylesford, and then his physical appearance and his personal history. They gave Philip a life as a soldier during the English Civil War in the seventeenth century. Following an affair with a Gypsy who was burned at the stake, Philip committed suicide in 1654.

The group, under the direction of A.R.G. and Iris Owen, met regularly for seances, at which they collectively visualized Philip and attempted to communicate with him. For months nothing happened. Then the group tried table-tilting, a technique in which participants place their fingertips lightly on a tabletop and invite spirits to communicate by levitating the table or rapping upon it. Table-tilting was a popular seance activity during the heyday of Spiritualism in the nineteenth and early twentieth centuries, and it was commonly believed that spirits created the effects. However, British psychologist Kenneth J. Batcheldor more recently theorized that those PK effects could be induced because of an atmosphere of belief and expectation on the part of the participants.

Once the Toronto group began table-tilting, Philip began communicating by moving the table and rapping out answers to questions. The personality identified himself as Philip, and correctly answered questions about himself as he had been created. He could not, however, answer questions beyond the history that had been constructed for him. Experiments with Philip went on for several years, and the group believed they had successfully formed a personality out of their collective subconscious. They called it "PK by committee." While some in the group believed that with sufficient effort they could create a physical manifestation of Philip, interest waned and work eventually stopped.

It is possible, then, that Mary and Eva contributed subconsciously to Devon and the Choir by believing in them and by *wanting* to believe in them. Their own thoughts may have added energy to a collective thought-form taking shape.

But the causes of poltergeist activity cannot always

be found among the living, and many cases on record have defied natural explanation. Ian Stevenson, a noted psychical researcher and a psychiatrist at the University of Virginia, has proposed that the theory of poltergeists as spirits of the dead should be given more attention by researchers. Spirit cases are characterized by meaningful communication and not by meaningless raps, as is often the case in living-agent instances. Physical phenomena in these instances are not limited to the presence of one person, and the movement of objects is more deliberate and not aimless. Finally, relief comes not through psychotherapy, but through exorcism, placation, or intercession. In the case of Devon and the Choir, most of the activity took place in Ann's presence—but did begin to occur around Eva when Ann and the others were not present. The movement of objects seemed deliberate: the throwing of newspaper wads, the turning on of the tape recorder, the playing of "Greensleeves," and the turning of the Josephine bust. It isn't known how Mary and Ann dealt with the trouble, but Eva obtained relief through a self-made exorcism of distance and psychological severance.

Some phenomena in the case resist explanation. For example, the bats that invaded Eva's home suggest the possibility of a supernatural interference. The most interesting puzzle of all is the cause of Ann's wounded and bleeding neck. The late Nandor Fodor might have suggested unconscious self-mutilation, as he did concerning Mrs. Forbes in the Thornton Heath case. However, the appearance of strange wounds also occurs in cases of demonic attack and possession that have been documented through the centuries. Since

Ann did seem to be psychically open as a result of her upbringing in magic and the use of psychic power, perhaps she was an easy target for malign entities. These entities in turn may have fed off the inner fantasies and fears of all three girls.

The truth may never be known.

Chapter Eight

Psychic Vampires

VAMPIRISM DOES NOT ALWAYS INVOLVE THE TAKING OF blood. The term "psychic vampirism" is used to describe the siphoning off of a person's energy and vitality, perhaps to the point where health is impaired. As we saw in Chapter Three, many of the early cases of vampirism recorded in Serbia involved a draining of vitality and not blood.

In occultism, psychic vampirism allegedly can be accomplished either by living persons or by supernatural entities. The purpose of psychic vampirism—also called psychic attack—is to weaken, debilitate, and destroy; to bend the will of the victim so that he obeys the attacker; or simply to draw off energy needed by the attacker. The victim feels fatigued or exhausted. In extreme cases, the victim falls ill and may even die.

Occult lore holds that living persons either naturally have the ability to psychically vampirize or have acquired it through magical training. Most often, they are said to drain persons in close physical proximity to them, but also purportedly can do so at a distance through magic. They project their will or allegedly travel out-of-body to attack in their invisible astral forms. In some cases, they are alleged to command supernatural beings to attack and drain the victim. The supernatural beings either are spirits or demons conjured by magic, or are artificial spirits, called "thought-forms," which are created by magic rituals for the purpose of attacking a specific victim.

Supernatural entities also are said to sometimes act on their own in attacking the living, as we saw in the hag cases in Chapter Three.

In this chapter, we shall take a look at a variety of encounters that appear to be types of psychic vampirism. We'll begin with the experiences of Dion Fortune (1890–1946), the renowned occultist and magician who rose to fame in England's great ceremonial magic circles. Fortune's own experience as the victim of psychic vampirism, and her observances of victims and perpetrators, led her to become the still-reigning authority on the subject.

We'll also look at the reputed psychic vampire war of two of Fortune's contemporaries in ceremonial magic, Samuel Liddell MacGregor Mathers and Aleister Crowley. Then, a woman from California tells the story of her encounter with a man adept at psychically vampirizing the living, and a man from Pennsylvania relates his encounter with an unseen vampirizing force that sapped his vitality for months.

The Distress of Dion Fortune

Dion Fortune had her first encounter with psychic attack as a young woman of twenty. She took a job working for a woman who had extensive occult knowledge learned during a residency in India. The woman controlled her staff with techniques of mind power, and a number of her employees suffered mysterious breakdowns. Fortune herself became the object of mind manipulation when her boss wanted her to give testimony in a lawsuit. The testimony contradicted Fortune's direct knowledge of the events surrounding the suit, and she resisted. But after spending time in the presence of her boss, who gave her an intense gaze and directed her what to say, Fortune became so dazed and exhausted that she was forced to retire to bed, where she slept for fifteen straight hours. During a second session with her boss, she found herself agreeing to baseless charges. This session also was followed by extreme exhaustion and dead sleep.

When Fortune decided to terminate her employment, her boss used the same technique to try to break her will. "You are incompetent, and you know it. You have no self-confidence and you have got to admit it," the woman said. Fortune denied this. Her boss kept up this litany for four hours. "I entered her room at ten o'clock, and I left it at two," Fortune wrote years later. "She must have said these two phrases several hundreds of times. I entered it a strong and healthy girl. I left it a mental and physical wreck and was ill for three years."

Fortune's experience caused her to research occultism to determine what had happened to her, and how she could have defended herself against it. "My body was like an electric battery that had been completely discharged," she wrote. "It took a long time to charge up again, and every time it was used before charging was completed, it ran down again rapidly. For a long time I had no reserves of energy, and after the least exertion would fall into a dead sleep at any hour of the day."

Her researches led her to conclude that damage had been sustained by her etheric double. The etheric double is said to be a nonphysical replica of the body that is attached to the body and helps channel the universal life-force to it. It is part of the aura, or invisible energy field, said to surround the body. Some psychics say they can see the aura and etheric body, and that symptoms of illness and disease are evident in the etheric body, manifesting there before appearing in the physical body. Fortune believed that the damage to her etheric double, caused by this woman, created a leak in her life-force. Thus she suffered profound exhaustion and mental fatigue.

Fortune's turnaround came in 1919 when she was initiated into an occult order. She became a respected occultist and adept in ritual magic, and wrote a number of fiction and nonfiction books about the occult. One of her best-known works is *Psychic Self-Defence* (1930), from which the preceding quotes were taken.

Her real name was Violet Firth, but Dion Fortune was the pen name chosen from her magical motto, *Deo non fortuna* ("By God, not chance"). It came from the Alpha and Omega Lodge of the Stella Matutina, the occult order she joined. The Stella

Matutina was an outer order of the renowned Hermetic order of the Golden Dawn, the greatest, albeit short-lived, Western magical order in modern times. The Golden Dawn boasted such occult luminaries as Samuel Liddell MacGregor Mathers, Aleister Crowley, William Butler Yeats, Arthur Edward Waite, and Israel Regardie. MacGregor Mathers and Crowley had a falling-out, and Crowley was ejected from the order. He retaliated with psychic attack, and he and MacGregor Mathers reputedly waged fierce warfare on the astral plane, sending armies of demons to attack each other.

Fortune's writings on psychic attack and vampirism stand today as classics in the field of occultism. From her own experiences, she gained firsthand knowledge of how psychic attacks occur, their symptoms in unsuspecting victims, and how the attacks can be warded off or nullified.

"I am of the opinion that psychic attacks are far commoner than is generally realised, even by occultists themselves," she stated. She acknowledged that getting people to admit such attacks was not easy because of skepticism and fear of seeming to be mentally unbalanced.

She said most people are normally protected from falling victim to psychic attack because of the vitality of their own protective energy fields, and their inability to perceive the invisible forces of the unseen. However, there are four conditions under which this protective veil can be rent, said Fortune: 1) being in a place where occult forces are concentrated; 2) encountering people who are adept at handling these forces; 3) dabbling in the occult and getting out of one's depth; and 4) falling victim to certain pathological conditions.

An attack can occur at any time, but most occur at night, and especially when the victim is sleeping, because those are times when psychic resistance is lowest. Phases of the moon also are important: The waning moon and dark of the moon are considered to be the best times for the working of harmful magic.

Symptoms of an attack are varied and include unexplained behavior, disturbed dreams, the hag syndrome, repulsive smells, exhaustion, confusion, dizziness, mental breakdown, illness, and the occurrence of poltergeist phenomena. In some cases, victims have shown bruises or tiny bite marks, which may bleed. Fortune, who believed herself to have been psychically attacked numerous times, awoke one morning with dried blood on her pillow from a small puncture behind the angle of the jaw. She attributed the puncture to the presence of a girl who was a psychic vampire. Others in the girl's proximity reported the same puncture marks and blood.

Fortune's help was sought by many who feared they were victims of occult attack. One case she cites in *Psychic Self-Defence* is that of Mr. C. and his first and second wives, who were victimized by Miss X. As a young girl, Miss X. had been engaged to a man who, soon after the engagement was announced, developed consumption and died of a violent hemorrhage. A few years later, she became engaged again, and the second fiancé also developed consumption. Although he, too, hemorrhaged, his illness was lingering, and he lived as an invalid for years. During his illness, Miss X. took a house, moved him in, and installed an aunt as chaperone. The aunt soon developed listlessness and for days at a stretch would lie unconscious. However, no cause of her illness could be found.

To break the tedium, Miss X. entertained herself by visiting Mr. and Mrs. C. She became infatuated with Mr. C., but her attentions went unrequited. Mrs. C. soon died of cancer of the womb. Much to the chagrin of Miss X., Mr. C. married another woman. The health of the second Mrs. C. also began to decline. She suffered nightmares, epilepticlike fits, weakness, and fatigue. Eventually she was diagnosed as having cancer of the womb. She, too, died.

At about the same time, Miss X.'s aunt and second fiancé also succumbed. Miss X. suffered a mental breakdown and was admitted to a nursing home in the country. In all likelihood, her vampirism finally turned on herself.

A Vampire Landlady

Another case to come out of modern England is reported in *The Psychology of Witchcraft* (1974) by Tom Ravensdale and James Morgan. It concerns a young woman and her husband who were offered accommodation by an older woman whom they knew slightly. Soon after moving in, the young woman began to feel uncomfortable because of the constant attention from the old landlady. Every evening she would be waiting for the girl to come home from work, and she would find a reason to visit the young woman when the husband was not present. She would fix the girl with an intense gaze. She seemed to emanate an unpleasant aura.

The young woman's energy declined and her health deteriorated. As she suffered, the old woman blossomed with vigor and vitality. The girl's husband suggested a change of residence, but the girl declined and opted instead to stay longer at work. As soon as she decreased the time spent in the landlady's house, her condition improved—and the old woman's deteriorated. Within a week or two, the old woman was bedridden. Unfortunately, the girl took pity on her and took to caring for her. The old woman's health improved immediately, but the girl's health declined to the point where her husband sent her to a doctor. The doctor diagnosed her as anemic and overworked, and ordered her to rest and eat a better diet. She followed his instructions, but made no improvement. Instead, she steadily grew worse and suffered from complete exhaustion and severe headaches.

Then the husband noticed two small red patches on her throat. The marks didn't hurt and were of unknown cause, so they were ignored.

The old woman, meanwhile, had become so rejuvenated and youthful-looking that she decided to take a trip into the country to visit relatives. During her absence, the girl's health returned. She decided to consult a psychic. The psychic clairvoyantly saw the old woman as a psychic vampire surrounded by an aura of evil, and advised the girl and her husband to depart the house immediately. Unfortunately, they lacked the funds to do so.

When the old woman returned, the girl's health once again declined. She was so weakened that she was hospitalized. Her red marks returned and began to bleed. A Spiritualist friend visited and recommended that the girl wear a crucifix and a ring blessed by a priest, and have her room sealed with holy water. The terrified girl agreed. When these measures had been taken, she experienced an immediate and marked improvement in her condition.

The "vampire" in turn became furious and displayed an uncontrolled hatred toward the girl. As the girl became stronger, the old woman weakened. At last the girl and her husband were able to move out. She made a complete recovery.

Unintentional Vampires

Not all cases of psychic vampirism are perpetrated by a calculating and malevolent individual. Some people seem to be unwitting energy vampires. Fortune, whose occult study was coupled with a study of psychoanalysis, found some clinic cases to be unusually exhausting. A nurse informed her that these same patients had an extraordinary capacity to absorb high voltages of electricity from the various therapy machines in use at the time.

We've all encountered individuals from time to time who leave us inexplicably wrung out and tired. They go spinning along like little psychic tornadoes, sucking up everyone in their paths and tossing them out drained and limp. Quite often it's impossible to pinpoint exactly what it is about such persons that makes being in their presence so exhausting. It's rarely anything specifically they do or say. These unwitting psychic vampires often are bright and cheerful people. They have boundless energy—because they've borrowed *yours*.

Psychic vampires who deliberately prey upon others learn their techniques through occult study. They want magical power in order to achieve whatever they desire, and they believe that stealing the life-force of others will help them obtain this power. They also want to manipulate others to bend to their will, and drawing off the life-force weakens a victim's will and resistance to domination.

A Psychic Duel

Perhaps the most famous story of psychic vampirism is the occult warfare waged by Aleister Crowley and Samuel Liddell MacGregor Mathers, mentioned earlier in this chapter. It is said that these two highly skilled magicians prepared themselves for months with magical procedures and rites in order to create vampiric thought-forms programmed to attack his human enemy.

The warfare reportedly was initiated by Mathers in 1890 when he created and sent a thought-form vampire to attack Crowley. Instead, Crowley, who was undoubtedly of superior magical skill, took the thought-form, made it nastier, and sent it back to attack Mathers. This warfare supposedly went on for years and was chronicled by journalists around the world. Mathers's health declined as the attacks continued. When Mathers succumbed in 1918, his widow blamed his death on Crowley's psychic vampirism. Prior to his death, Mathers once described the awful nature of the thought-form vampire:

Only the upper portions of its body were visible when it would appear. Obviously female, it had narrow breasts protruding through some kind of dark raiment. Below the waist nothing existed. The curious eyes were deep-socketed, and glowed faintly with an intense coral-colored luminosity. The head was flat, set low between white, blubbery shoulders, as though it were cut off just below those fearful 'eyes.' Like tiny useless flippers, the arms seemed almost vestigial. They were like unformed limbs, still in the fetal stage.

But the thing didn't need arms. Its terrifying weapon was an extraordinarily long, coated gray tongue. Tube-like and hollow, it bore a small orbicular hole at its tip, and that lascivious tongue kept darting snake-like in and out of a circular, lipless mouth. Always trying to catch me off guard it would suddenly strike at me, like a greedy missile, attempting to suck out my auric vitality.

Perhaps the being's most terrifying feature was its absolutely loathsome habit of trying to cuddle up like a purring cat, rubbing its half-materialized form against me, all the while alert, hoping to find a gap in my defenses. And when it was sometimes successful—I was not always prepared nor strong enough to maintain the magical barriers—it would pierce my aura with that wicked tongue right down to my naked skin, causing a most painful sensation. This was followed by a total enervation of my body and spirit for a week or more. A listless, dread experience. (Hillyer, *Vampires*)

Was Crowley capable of creating such an insidious vampire, or was this a delusion on the part of Mathers? Individuals who met Crowley, even those skeptical of the magical arts, came away profoundly impressed with the indescribable power and energy they sensed emanating from him. His residences were pervaded by an atmosphere of evil that seemed to affect all who visited. Crowley, who delighted in calling himself the Antichrist, the Beast of the Apocalypse, and the Lord of the New Aeon, reportedly turned his power on anyone who crossed him. A butcher who once pestered him over unpaid bills inexplicably chopped through a femoral artery and died after Crowley purportedly wrote a demon's name on one of the bills.

Vincent Hillyer, an author and adventurer whom we will meet later in Chapter Ten, knew the novelist W. Somerset Maugham, who had witnessed some of Crowley's magical feats firsthand. In the early part of the twentieth century, Maugham for a time shared an apartment in Paris with Crowley and Allan Bennett. Crowley terrified Maugham. He served as the model for the black-magician Oliver Haddo in Maugham's novel *The Magician*.

"Crowley was such a strange person," Maugham told Hillyer. "I saw that man do things there was no logical or scientific explanation for. One time we were walking down the street in Paris and I asked him to show me something that he could do to prove that he did have powers. Crowley pointed to a man walking halfway down the block and said, 'See that fellow? I'll make him trip.' He said something indistinguishable or motioned in some way, and the man tripped and looked around surprised, as though he didn't know what he'd tripped over. Another time I saw Crowley make a man entirely disappear in a pillar of salt. The man just dissolved and was gone. Crowley had something about his aura that if you came within a couple of feet of the man, you felt this premonition of fear and you did not want to touch him, ever. I was deathly afraid of that man. I never did anything to anger him. He was the only person I ever met in my entire life that I was deathly afraid of."

Crowley's fascination with blood, torture, and sexual degradation was well known during his lifetime. He sharpened his teeth so that he could give blood-drawing "Serpent Kisses" to his "Scarlet Women," followers who participated in his magical rites.

Few reports of psychic vampirism can match the sensational detail of the Crowley-Mathers confrontation, or even the episodes of Dion Fortune. However, interesting and dramatic cases do occur. The following two stories demonstrate markedly different circumstances and characteristics of psychic vampirism.

He Gets What He Wants

Jayne [not her real name] lives in California, where she met a man who, she discovered, seemed to prey upon others by draining their energy and manipulating their will. Here is her account in her own words:

I know a "psychic vampire," for want of a better term. He can achieve almost any goal he desires, as long as he can use other people to do it. He can attract people to whatever goal he sets, even against their own will. He draws "energy" off of other people to protect himself and keep from getting sick—and they feel drained or listless after he's done so. I know him very well, and he is not using any form of magic, witchcraft, or occult science. I do, which is why I've had a chance to observe him closely over a number of years without becoming victimized. It seems that crystals and visualization prevent his power from manifesting. A friend of mine says she believes he is simply being used by a discarnate entity, or even a demon, but I don't accept that, since whatever he goes after is always for his own personal material gain. I believe he is an evil man who didn't become what he is purely by accident.

I live in a small town in northern California. Pat [not his real name] moved here about four and a half years ago. Physically, his build is average, under six feet tall. He is in his mid-forties, with dark hair and eyes, of European descent. He has a young son. At first, I took no notice of him, but he went out of his way to insure that we ran into each other. He later bragged about this, telling me that he'd made up his mind that we would be "together" after seeing me walk to our local post office. I later discovered that he had done this before in other places. It is his usual method.

His story was that he'd been a "hell-raiser" all of his life, but after receiving custody of his son from his ex-wife, he decided to settle down. We started seeing each other. My mother and two of my friends, all deeply religious people, took an instant dislike to Pat. I did not—something rare for me, as I usually pick up vibes from people very easily. Soon I began to observe some strange things. He called himself a loner, yet he was always seeking people out, especially women with children, just for conversation, and would sometimes spend literally *hours* at our local park talking. I'll admit that my first thought was that he was a liar and a womanizer. Next I noticed that when he had a very real need for some material item, someone would give it to him. In conversation, he made it sound as if it were some kind of casual gift. Then I observed that he never got sick. Indeed, he brags that this is his own doing, saying, "Other people get sick, *I* don't." A sudden thing, like food poisoning, he throws off in a matter of hours—more quickly if someone is present. I thought he was a little crazy the first time I saw him insist on going to someone's house even though he was suddenly taken ill. Interestingly, he was born with an inherited disease that allows him to collect a pension instead of working, yet the disease is not apparent in him. But in his family, it is crippling. I got to know several members of his family who have it. The disease causes a progressive deterioration of the body that is either crippling or fatal. It cannot be treated.

I began to notice that, while Pat was friendly with all classes of people, those he hung out with were ex-cons, bikers, people who did dope and drank a lot, and women who were, for want of a better term, loose. He didn't have sex with them—but he seemed to almost *require* that they be sexually interested in him.

After several months, we became lovers, and because he believed that I was in love with him—at the time, I was—he confided to me that the source of his "power" was a form of mind control he'd studied, combined with the martial art aikido. He told me, "If you can control your own mind, you can control other people's minds." Aikido, if you aren't familiar with the martial arts, teaches its students how to draw energy from other people and use it for their own purposes. I believe that Pat perverted the teaching of aikido to his own personal use in order to achieve personal control over others.

I first became suspicious of him when I went with him to a mutual friend's house. This friend had a tire that Pat wanted for his car. I watched him manipulate our friend in three steps. I have since verified his technique by watching him use it on other people. First, he made physical contact, such as shaking hands, arm around the shoulder, etc. Second, he looked *directly* into our friend's eyes. I've noticed people are unable to break his gaze. Third, he began to speak in a low, personal, confident manner. He paid our friend a compliment and generally had him believing that *they* wanted to do Pat a favor. Afterward, the person—I hesitate to use the word "victim" since they cooperate and want so much to please him—almost visibly sagged, as if a powerful force had let him go, and Pat moved away.

Gradually, I realized what he was doing in the park: drawing energy, i.e., "feeding." I discovered that he had developed the ability to believe whatever he said. That was why I couldn't get bad vibes off of him when he told me that he wanted to make a fresh start—he did, and he had convinced himself, in order to convince me, and anyone else. I've seen him do this hundreds of times—decide that he needs or wants something, tell himself whatever lie to make it possible, and then tell it to others. And believe me, they *are* convinced, in spite of evidence to the contrary. They wind up thinking that they're the ones who are mistaken.

I know several people who've told me what a "tiring

person" Pat is to be around. My mother and best friend, as I mentioned before, believe him to be both evil and a psychic vampire. But, by and large, most people enjoy his company. He's understated, can be amusing, and treats everyone the same.

He has a sinister side, and I've seen him try to use the energy to cause psychic harm to others. He drains to cause psychic harm to others, he seduces people against their better judgment into doing things they wouldn't do without his influence. He loves to spend time around children because, I would imagine, their energy level is so intense, and uses his son to be in their company. My suspicions were confirmed the first time his son's mother returned, after some absence, and took him for visitation. Pat became listless.

Indirectly, harm literally follows him wherever he goes— suicides, marital troubles, arrests. One small incident comes immediately to mind. He gave his son a cat, and grew very tired of having to deal with it. He kept saying how he wished he was rid of it, and one night a weasel killed it. He got into an argument with a man and his wife over some money that he thought the man owed him, and the man had a heart attack a week later. I know these kinds of things are circumstantial.

Finally, I had physical evidence myself, when he actually tried to "drain" me against my will one evening because I told him that something he planned to do was evil, and he got very angry. When he tried to drain me he was, first of all, very agitated—he was angry at his ex-wife. He told me that he was thinking of actually doing physical harm to her, and bragged that there was nothing I could do about it. It later turned out he was wrong. He became very upset with me because I didn't see the matter exactly his way. He started talking about what a terrible person she was, and seemed to become more excited the more he talked, trying to convince me to see his viewpoint.

His appearance took on a "desperate-forceful" look. His eyes were powerful-looking, as though all of his will was concentrated behind them. I do know that at that moment he wanted me to agree with him more than anything in the world, although even under ordinary circumstances, he dislikes having anyone disagree with him. I assume his desperation was prompted by what he knew would happen if his ex-wife spent more time with their child. Because his anger was so sudden, I didn't have a chance to protect myself. But I was fortunate in that I recognized what he was doing when he began to drain me.

I felt a sudden loss of energy, the temptation to say "what the hell" to myself and agree with him, taking the path of least resistance. I even, for a moment, thought that I might be wrong. I became very tired, and his words just flowed over me. I then got up and I went into the bathroom to collect my thoughts.

When I went back into the dinette, he was going through some legal papers, and I started to "read" a book, chanting silently to myself. I often chant mantras to center my being. I was still terribly tired, but he didn't try to convince me anymore. I think he knew, when I was able to stand up and walk away from him, that he was defeated. I never mentioned it, or let him know in any way that he'd had the power to drain some of my life-force. I also was never in his company again without first surrounding myself with light.

I want to point out that I was never, at any time, afraid, however. I saw him as a fundamentally weak person who had to draw psychic energy from other people in order to survive, while the rest of us draw it from the universe. Occasionally, Pat tried to convince me of something or tried to get me to do something—what in an ordinary person would be termed "persuasion"—but he always backed down with a couple of firm "no's." It was as if he'd met his match, and I knew it.

I believe, sometimes, that he was drawn to the light that surrounds me, like moths are drawn to lamplight. He hungered for something he could never attain. This is only an attempt at finding a reason, not an excuse for him. He was exposed many times, by life, by others, and by myself, to the right path—and he wasn't interested.

Our relationship ended because I made *him* believe that I wasn't the woman he'd fallen in love with. I made myself obnoxious, so that he wouldn't want to be around me, and let him believe that he made the choice to split up. It was the safest way to avoid any psychic ill will directed at me personally, especially since he still lives in this area.

I didn't learn to protect myself from psychic vampirism per se. I am a student of the occult, and I am knowledgeable about forms of protection against *any* psychic attack. I practice meditation, chanting, visualization, and the use of crystals and other stones. I also believe in prayer. I don't espouse any particular system, and am very much against following any one path blindly. For instance, a friend of mine uses candle-burning rituals regularly. This doesn't work for me, but it doesn't mean that they don't work for her.

The main thing for anyone to remember is that a psychic vampire draws energy. Once he is not able to do so, he will leave you alone—unless you are, as I was, the object of his obsession, but I dealt with that. You can shut yourself down, so to speak, by simply walking away. Or by focusing on something mundane, like the pattern in the carpet. It has to be something like that—something that arouses no interest whatsoever on your part—because interest energizes you, and he will draw off of it. People who don't know what a mantra is can chant the names of family members over and over, or even the months of the year in order. Key words: Bore yourself.

You can't protect someone else from them, however. For example, people who come under Pat's influence do so of their own free will—*he* makes them want to do what *he* wants them to do—and *their* free will cannot be interfered with. Therefore, I've had to stand by and watch him manipulate people I've known for years without being able to help.

The "Thing" That Came in the Night

Bob, a native of Pennsylvania, is average in height, slender, and appears to be much younger than his forty years. He often seems nervous, and perhaps it's because he's a bit of a psychic lightning rod. In early childhood, Bob was aware of the presence of ghosts in the houses where his family lived. He has an unusual degree of empathy, and can often feel the thoughts and emotions of others inside of him. If the emotions are hostile, he can feel invaded and used. At times in his adult life, he has visited sites and houses said to be haunted—and inexplicable or poltergeistlike phenomena always seem to happen as a result.

In the mid-1970s, he had a brief but intense and empathetic relationship with a woman who seemed caught up in a terrible psychic drama beyond her control. Bob became the victim of an apparent vampiric entity or force that attacked him over and over again, nearly wrecking his health and his life.

I met Bob one snowy winter afternoon in New York City at a meeting of the New York Fortean Society, a rather fitting setting. Forteans share a passion for unexplained phenomena and anomalies, such as Bigfoot, rains of frogs, ghosts, and UFOs. The society takes its name from Charles Fort (1874–1932), an American journalist who devoted his retirement to collecting clippings and information about such phenomena.

I set up an interview with Bob for a later date. He lives in Wilkes-Barre, Pennsylvania, and agreed to return to Manhattan for an afternoon. The day before his arrival, I made arrangements to conduct the interview in a room at a private library in the city. When Bob and I arrived at the library, the building was uncomfortably hot. Our host apologized, saying the heat was inexplicably out of control. We were sent to an office where an air conditioner blasted away but made no significant impact on the sweaty heat for the several hours that we were there.

On our way out, we encountered our host again. He gave me a keen look and said, "Didn't you say you were writing a book on ghosts or vampires or something like that?"

"That's right," I said.

"Well, this *is* strange," our host said. "Right after you called to reserve the room yesterday, that's when the heat came on and we couldn't get it turned off. We thought the thermostat was broken. Now that you're leaving, the heat has gone off by itself."

I'm accustomed to odd things happening during the course of my research of the paranormal, and I was amused by the thought that perhaps Bob and I were part of this phenomenon. But Bob looked disconcerted. Psychic lightning once again.

It was difficult for Bob to talk about the vampire attacks, for strong emotions about that period in his life still ride close to the surface. His empathetic ability was a significant factor in his psychic vulnerability to the attacks.

Empathy is the tuning in on an intuitive or psychic level to the emotions, moods, and attitudes of another person, and understanding and absorbing them without verbal communication. Empathy is neither entirely conscious nor entirely unconscious, but falls somewhere in between. It can occur over a long distance, as though feelings and thoughts are being transmitted telepathically. Empaths are particularly susceptible to depression, feelings of suffering and distress, and negative emotions such as hostility, anger, and hatred. Empaths can sometimes feel the physical pains and discomforts of another, though the degree of empathy varies by individual. Some empaths are walking psychic sponges, picking up whatever they're exposed to. Others experience empathy only with those to whom they have close emotional ties. Twins are the most likely to share empathy with each other.

Bob is an identical twin. "We're not that close, but sometimes I can hear him in my head," he explained. "It's like an intrusion. I can experience other people in the same way, though rarely. There was an occasion once when I was renting a room in a house that belonged to a young couple. One night the husband went out drinking. I woke up when I heard him come up the driveway, but I quickly fell back asleep. In a few minutes I awoke again due to the sensation of being crowded into a small space, as if I were a sardine. I thought for a moment that someone had crawled into the bed, but I quickly discerned that that wasn't the case. I still felt cramped. Suddenly I heard the voice of the husband in my head say, 'Oh, shit!' and very abruptly the sensation of being 'squooshed' ceased. Apparently the husband had come in, gone to sleep, and in some nonphysical way had occupied my body, perhaps mistaking it for his own. Who knows! I usually don't experience other people so completely."

Bob's "near-fatal psychic attraction" began, innocently enough, in church. "She went to the same church as I did," he said. "It was a small church in the Poconos, and the denomination wasn't mainstream. People came from a wide area to attend. Often I would get a ride with Gwen [a pseudonym] from the Wilkes-Barre area, and we got to know each other fairly well. Consequently we got into the habit of confiding in each other to some degree, particularly in terms of our reactions to some of the teachings of the church, which was of the fundamentalist viewpoint.

We were trying pretty hard to meet the requirements of what we thought God wanted, while at the same time experiencing some degree of confusion about what we could expect from Him. I know the term 'Him' sounds a bit chauvinistic in the 1990s, but in the 1970s, God was always the Father or the Son, so to speak. So we would wonder, for instance, whether God would take the role of matchmaker: Was there somebody in the church whom God had called to be your mate in the course of your Christian development, or did He not involve Himself with such matters, so that you should find someone on your own? Questions like this often seemed to be unsatisfactorily answered while the clergy devoted their sermons to more mundane aspects of Christian living.

"I guess I would have to say that part of the reason that the question of what might be called 'the soulmate issue' was on my mind was that Gwen was a very attractive woman and I was rather fond of her, but she was dating other people at the time. I wondered if we were 'meant for each other' and if so, what I should do about it. I was somewhat resentful of her dating other people, though at first we weren't really dating; she was just my ride to church."

Bob went on to explain the course his association with Gwen took as time went on.

"At this point I have a bit of a problem trying to continue with an account of everything that happened. When I experienced these things it was the mid-1970s and I experienced them with the perspective I had at that time, which is not quite the way I see things now. At the same time, things seemed to happen in ways that I still cannot accept in an intellectual sense.

"I believe that in a sense, nothing happens that isn't in some way a version of 'you reap what you sow.' So I would be inclined to view these vampire attacks—or whatever you want to call them—as events that were karmically related to me, sort of like something Jane Roberts described in her book about Seth on one occasion."

Bob cited an experience described by author Jane Roberts, who became famous for her channeling of the nonphysical entity Seth in the 1960s and 1970s.

"In *The Seth Material,* Jane Roberts describes being attacked one night by a ghost, and Seth tells her the next day that it was her own creation," Bob said. "All the things she didn't like about herself and had tried to separate from herself had formed into an astral entity. That way she could hate it as if she were hating a separate being, but really she was still hating something that was a part of her. This entity hated being hated, so it attacked her. Seth explained that the attack also was her own energy trying to 'return home.'

"I'd have to say that in some ways my experiences fit that pattern, because in the course of events I did end up sending out a lot of anger. On the other hand, I had the experience of being 'bitten' by something that seemed to be very external, and which fits in more with the traditional concept of vampirism. This occurred at the beginning of about a decade of weird happenings in the Wilkes-Barre area. Whether or not what I experienced was a part of the overall weirdness, I'll never know, but I'll try to include it for the sake of perspective.

"The Wyoming Valley, in which Wilkes-Barre sits, was a rather strange place in the period from about

1977 until about 1987. There seemed to be ghosts all over the place in one form or another. In October of 1979 the local newspaper ran a Halloween article about a house in town that it dubbed 'Wilkes-Barre's own Amityville Horror.'

"The residents of the house were tormented by ghostly visitors knocking on the door, sitting on the porch, levitating the children, wailing all night, and carrying on in various and sundry other ways until one night an ancient doll with a human face and moving eyes hovered over the bed of the owners, and they fled with the children in tow.

"In the early '80s, people in the area were awakening to find strange people in their bedrooms in the middle of the night. The local talk radio station received calls about people's experiences with a black figure that became known as 'the black specter.' A woman described biting the finger of a man she found standing next to her bed one night. She said it was 'like biting into rotten celery.'

"The weirdness seemed to come to a head in the late '80s with the experiences of the Jack Smurl family, who lived eight miles out of Wilkes-Barre. Mr. Smurl is supposed to have been raped by a ghostly old hag with red eyes and glowing green teeth. I certainly didn't experience anything as vivid as that, thank God! But whatever I may have brought onto myself by my own virtue or lack of virtue, the fact remains that things were pretty strange in the area at that time.

"What happened in my own case was that I found out that Gwen was experiencing a lot of stress related to her home life. Members of her immediate family counted on her to provide a source of income for them, and at the same time they fought among themselves constantly. I'm talking about adults, not children. She wanted to be free of them for her own peace of mind. She wanted to get her own apartment, but felt that she couldn't afford to do it while she was supporting them.

"At the same time, her boss was giving her a hard time at work, and one of her boyfriends was pressuring her to abandon her family and marry him. She tried to accommodate everybody as best she could.

"Since that time I have heard of a psychological condition brought on by stress wherein a person suffers bouts of paralysis at night. I think she was experiencing this.

"When a person is going through this stress syndrome, they awaken from sleep but find that they are paralyzed. In a while the condition passes, but I guess it can be very frightening. She told me she would sense the impulse to awaken, but have to fight her way out of the dream state. In order to wake up, she would have to imagine that she was making her hands into a fist and then, to use her words, 'it was like punching my way through a brick wall.' Then, when she was able to create a bit of movement, she was able to open her eyes and come out of the dream state. She could move only very slowly at first, and she did mention that it often felt, in the initial stages, as if there was someone sitting on her chest.

"It was this last part, that it felt like there was someone sitting on her chest, that disturbed me."

"I can see that it might!" I said.

Bob continued, "Remember that at that time, we were going to this fundamentalist church and were always hearing Scriptures like the one that goes: 'The Devil goes around like a roaring lion, seeking whom he may devour.' It seemed to me that maybe she was being attacked by a devil at night. I hadn't heard of the psychological condition, the stress-related paralysis, at that time."

Bob went on to explain that he may have added to Gwen's stress.

"I began to get very angry at this stage of the game. I was mad at her family for not letting her live in peace; I was mad at her boyfriend who seemed to be driving her crazy with his demands that she marry him. I was mad at our pastor, because I had told him about what she'd said about being paralyzed at night, and he didn't seem to care. He said something like, 'Well, maybe she'll come speak to me about it.' And here she was, being eaten alive by demons, for heaven's sake! That's how I felt.

"And I really began to hate her boyfriend, whom she hadn't told anything about the paralysis because she didn't think he'd understand and she didn't want him to think she was crazy.

"So it was obviously up to me to get to the bottom of all this, or so I thought. She liked that idea, too, for a while, and we would go on dates to talk things over, about twice a week. I really wanted to be sure she was all right, and I was starting to feel quite fond of her—which, unfortunately, raised her stress level to new heights, because, you see, now she had *two* demanding boyfriends to deal with."

At this point, Bob said, strange things began to happen.

"Gwen decided that she would try to handle the paralysis on her own. She figured that, with God's help, she could learn to live with whatever was happening, and besides, she let me know, the paralysis attacks always seemed to occur after she had been with me. She angrily accused me of being the oppressing entity. 'I think it's you!' she exclaimed in a tone of voice that left no doubt that she was wise to my tricks.

"It was me! I was the Devil. I was Satan! I was crushed. I was hurt.

"I wondered if it *was* me. I wondered if I was some sort of nocturnal vampire. Maybe I really went around attacking people at night on the astral plane, as I would say now. In the 1970s, I had never heard of the astral plane. But then *I* started being attacked at night, too!

"My feeling now is that it was similar to what happened to Jane Roberts. I had been getting very angry. At night I would go to sleep, and sleep peacefully for a while—about an hour or an hour and a half. I guess that this represented the time I was recovering from the exhaustion that accumulates from a day's activities. Anyway, I would be fast asleep when all of a sudden I would feel a cloud of intense anger descend into my body. That's what it felt like, something external entering through my back, or descending into my body.

"The anger would be so intense that there was no civil way to deal with it. I would be wide awake instantly. I would leap out of bed, cursing and swearing in a loud voice. I would punch anything I could. Tables, chairs, walls. Bureaus. Nothing was safe. Fortunately, I lived in a small rented room at the time. After a few seconds my strength would be gone. I would literally crawl back into bed, punch the pillow once or twice for good measure, and pass out into a deep sleep. In this weakened condition, in the period of time that it took to crawl into bed and pass into oblivion, I would feel great sorrow and a desperate wish for soothing feminine energy. I would imagine that I was in Gwen's arms, and truly, I felt as if her energy was around me as I dozed off. The attacks on me got to the point where they came twice a week at their worst. At first, they came only on nights after I had seen her, and then they came even if I hadn't seen her, perhaps because I was sort of mentally with her." Bob added, "I think I really was a vampire."

"You mean a psychic vampire?" I asked.

Bob nodded. "In the time that has passed since all these events, I have become familiar with a number of concepts that relate to how human energy exists in nonphysical states, such as the aura and out-of-body experiences. If human thought and mental energy are not bound by distance, as is suggested by the phenomenon of ESP, and if astral travel is possible, then energy stealing and disruption are certainly possible, as well as healing and curative techniques. A person could be a psychic vampire instead of a blood-drinking vampire, and he wouldn't need to have fangs or hide in a coffin during the day.

"It is my understanding that all of us have an aura of energy around us that is 'our' energy. If we are under stress, drink heavily or do drugs, or lack physical nourishment, our auras 'leak.' If your aura is leaking energy, you might be inclined to cozy up to someone who has energy to spare so that the 'hole' in your aura can seal itself, or so that you can simply borrow another person's energy to keep your own energy level up.

"Looking back at what was happening to us, I can see all kinds of possibilities. Gwen was under a lot of stress. Stress supposedly can cause energy loss through the aura. Presumably enough of an energy loss in this manner could result in moments of paralysis due to a total loss of energy. A person in this condition might feel 'half dead.'

"Anger, which I was feeling, is reported to appear in the aura as something like bloody red lightning bolts —how appropriate—that blast holes through the aura on their way out and in, while sexual energy can be beneficial or detrimental depending on whether it is in the nature of lust, a depletion, or love. Although I was fond of Gwen, we did not have sex because of our church's teaching that sex was allowable only in marriage. I can't say that sexual energy wasn't involved in our relationship, however.

"No doubt with the anger I was experiencing, I was blasting away my own energy supply, as well as depleting it sexually and in the course of my daily existence. Perhaps, if there was mutual power-vampirizing going on, with all the mixed emotions and love triangles that were involved here, clouds of energy loss—so to speak—coupled with destructive red bolts of anger, could have combined to form an energy-depleting glob of negative energy that attacked me at night. It would have been something I helped create out of my own energy supply, like Jane Roberts's hostile ghost, but it wouldn't have been a real vampire in the traditional sense."

"Do you believe there are any 'real vampires'?" I asked.

Bob hesitated. "Actually, to be a real vampire you would have to be dead," he said. "I think there probably are such things as real vampires, and that they are what is called 'the living dead.' In the movies they are depicted as having fangs and all that. But they are really ghosts that 'live' in the bodies of buried corpses.

"I think that the red-eyed, green-fanged hag that was supposed to have attacked Jack Smurl might have been a real, dead vampire. But a person who is still alive in the flesh could be a sort of temporary vampire, too, since he could deplete you of vital energy to some degree. This would be a psychic vampire.

"This ties in with the rest of the story—the things that happened after Gwen said that I was causing her attacks. I think I was a psychic vampire for a while, but I may have had an encounter with a *real* one as well."

I asked Bob to explain what had happened.

"Gwen told me that she didn't want to see me anymore. Needless to say, I wasn't very happy about it, and I did try to pursue her for a while. My feeling was that it wasn't so much that she didn't like me, or thought that I was truly a vampire, but that she wanted to have some peace and quiet. I could understand that, but I wasn't ready to throw in the towel. I was genuinely fond of her, but didn't really know of any course of action that would be right to pursue. Eventually Gwen left the Wilkes-Barre area, partly, I'm sure, to get away from me.

"I felt terrible. Not only did I feel terrible because she was gone, I felt terrible because of the entire ordeal I had been through. I was totally exhausted. On top of everything else, I had spent a long time job hunting in the area after having graduated from community college, but I seemed to be unable to get any work in the area until after Gwen had gone."

At one point, Bob thought about visiting Gwen and "reclaiming" the relationship. The night he decided to do so, he was awakened from sleep by a large bat that had flown in his open window and seemed to be attacking him in swoops and dive-bombs. Bob jumped out of bed and fled the room. When he returned several minutes later, the bat was gone. Shaken, Bob took this as a sign that he should not pursue his plans. Was the bat attack a freak event, or could it possibly have been connected to his troubled relationship with Gwen? Bob said he was still uncertain. Nonetheless, it is similar to the bat encounter experienced by Eva in Chapter Seven, when she became swept up in some sort of supernatural force beyond her control.

Bob decided it was best for him to drop all contact with Gwen. "I ended up moving in with a friend," he said. "Joe [a pseudonym] was sharing an apartment with a friend of his, Bill. Bill was going to move out, but was still there when I first came, and didn't move out until a month later.

"While I was there, a number of things happened. I was able to secure a job at a nearby restaurant working nights from eleven to eight in the morning. That seemed to work out all right, but I had no reserves of energy at all. I would come home from work and sleep twelve to fourteen hours a day. I seemed to have no energy but to work, sleep, and eat. This condition lasted for the next five months, and only gradually did I get to the point of sleeping only nine hours a day. I was totally spent.

"When I first arrived at Joe's apartment, Bill had a pair of parakeets in a birdcage. They had always gotten along well, but after my arrival they began to fight with each other, and within a week one killed the other.

"Both Bill and Joe commented on how unusual it was that the birds had gotten along so well for such a long time and then become violent. They didn't say anything like, 'Things were fine until *you* came here,' but I was very much aware of the fact that that had been the case, and I seriously wondered if I was creating some sort of energy drain in the household.

"Another thing that happened was that Joe experienced what felt to him like a homosexual attack while he was sleeping. He is not gay, so he was quite startled by it. I am not gay, either, but I was the only other person in the room at the time of this event, and so I began to be concerned that there was a possibility that I had in some way been responsible for Joe's experience.

"I should make it clear that Joe was dreaming when the 'attack' took place, but he screamed when he dreamed it, and awoke immediately. He said that it felt 'quite real.' In light of my experience with the anger attacks, which had seemed to descend into my body as if they were an external force, I became quite concerned that I might have brought some sort of a ghost with me. But I didn't mention this to Joe at the time.

"In the years since that event, Joe and I have become good friends, and we have kidded about it on numerous occasions, but I was quite concerned about it at the time. I began to wonder if there was more to all that had been transpiring than I had considered. I began to wonder if I was in the company of a real vampiric spirit—something that wasn't part of me.

"I don't suppose I'll ever really know the answer to the question. I never saw anything while at Joe's apartment to indicate the presence of anything otherworldly, but I did have a curious experience after I had been there for about four months.

"Joe had quite a library, and I came across Dion Fortune's book *Psychic Self-Defence*. I was quite eager to learn what I could on the subject, and although the book had been written quite a while ago, it contained a lot of material that was new to me.

"Ms. Fortune explained that there *was* such a thing as psychic vampirism, and described how it worked. She claimed that a 'normal' person could sometimes be a vampire on the astral level. This is why it can be a draining experience to be in the presence of some people. Others, she said, were vampires by night, unbeknownst even to themselves: They had no waking knowledge that while out of the body during sleep, they were draining their friends, family, etc., of energy. Alcoholics might fit into this category, for instance. And then there were the real vampires: the Undead who maintained an earth plane existence in their astral bodies by feeding on those whose auras were leaking. Or by temporarily manifesting physically as a ghost does, and actually biting people, as is shown in the movies. A vampire bite, Ms. Fortune claimed, would resemble an insect bite to someone who had experienced it.

"Whether it was due to the power of suggestion, or something else, I cannot say, but about three days after reading Ms. Fortune's book, I was watching TV in Joe's apartment. It was an early spring afternoon, and the temperature outside was about sixty degrees. I had the windows open, and it was a sunny day. The time was about three o'clock. Because it was early spring—in April—there was no significant insect population, as is the case later in the summer.

"All of a sudden I felt a sharp sting, like a wasp sting, on my arm. I thought I had been stung, in fact, and was expecting to see an insect. Instead, there were no bugs to be found, but on my arm, right where the vein is that the Red Cross uses when they take blood donations—there were two little holes, as if I had taken a stapler and stapled myself! It really blew me away! The experience seemed to verify the reality of vampire attacks as Dion Fortune had described them. I was stunned. Perhaps there was something in the room that wanted me to know it was there, because I've never experienced anything like that since."

"Did you experience a loss of energy?" I asked.

"I had been feeling drained even before this took place, so I can't really say whether there was any effect," Bob replied.

Bob's life returned to a more normal style after the mysterious bite. There were no more vampire attacks, and his health returned in a few months.

Today he seems healthy and prosperous. He works in a nursing home, and still has an interest in things of a paranormal nature, but fortunately, as he puts it, not as an active participant.

Protection Against Psychic Vampirism

As seen from Jayne's story, there are prescriptions for dealing with the attacks of psychic vampires. Focusing on the mundane and trivial is one. Humor is another. Fortune says, "If the victim of an occult attack concentrates on mundane things, he is a heartbreaking proposition for any sorcerer. What is the sorcerer to do if, at the time when he is operating the Black art, his victim is at the local cinema roaring at the antics of Charlie Chaplin?"

Amulets worn to ward off evil, such as lucky charms, religious objects, and occult symbols, are also effective to the extent of your belief in them. It won't do you much good to wear a cross or a pentacle if you have no belief in the powers it represents and invokes. It's not the object itself that provides the protection, but the mental outlook it stimulates in you.

The same holds true for prayers. A prayer is a powerful means of communing with the Divine. Petitioning the Divine to intercede and protect is most effective when done with belief and, especially, a feeling of love, for love itself drives away the negative. The great healer Ambrose Worrall once observed that *all* thoughts are prayers. Worrall also said that the memorized prayers learned in religious practice are great mind cleansers.

In fact, any standardized prayer is a mantra. (*Mantra* is a Sanskrit term meaning "mind" and "to deliver.") It describes an association of syllables, ranging from a few to a thousand or more, that are chanted for spiritual or magical purpose. Mantras create mental pictures—they express what is and what comes to pass. Mantras are most common in Hinduism, but are used in many religions, such as Buddhism, Islam, Roman Catholicism, and Jainism. They are too complex in nature to be discussed here. Basically, their power derives from the awesome power of sacred sound, which exists everywhere in the universe and can both create and destroy. Mantras are used in the pursuit of enlightenment, and also as protection against evil and in the exorcism of demons. It's not wise to attempt to use unfamiliar mantras without the proper spiritual training, so stick with prayers you're familiar with.

Visualization is another powerful weapon in your defense arsenal. The idea is to visualize yourself enveloped in a brilliant white light that no evil can penetrate. As with amulets and prayers, the image must be fueled by your own strong *belief.*

According to Fortune, it helps to keep the stomach full, because the digestion of food blocks psychic operations. Also, soak up sunlight, which Fortune says helps to strengthen the aura. However, she cautioned, avoid going away to the country, the sea, or the mountains, as these are all places where psychic forces are stronger than in urban environments, which are rooted to the material plane. Above all, avoid solitude, and keep busy.

Finally, there is the old antivampire standby, garlic. To protect your house, strew garlic about, leave it overnight, and in the morning collect it and burn it. According to folklore, the garlic will have absorbed any noxious psychic emanations present. Onions may be substituted for garlic. You can also hang garlic over your bed or keep it on your person, although you needn't wear a wreath or garland of it as shown in some vampire films. Wrap a clove or bulb in foil and keep it in your pocket. Once again, the belief factor must come into play. A friend of mine once was informed by a woman who practiced magic that she had placed a curse on him. He began having hag attacks at night. Another friend advised him to defend himself by keeping a bit of wrapped garlic in his pocket. He did, and the hag attacks stopped. He later encountered the woman who'd cursed him. "You're wearing something, aren't you?" she demanded angrily. "I can't get through." After some time had elapsed, my friend removed the garlic. The attacks did not resume; apparently the sorceress had moved on to new territory.

It is difficult to assess cases of psychic vampirism because of their intangible nature, and because so much seems to depend upon the psychological state of the individuals involved. However, these encounters, especially those involving unseen attacking agents like the vampires in Chapter Seven, come close to the ideal vampire encounter I defined at the outset of my research. They involve attacks by an agent upon the living to torment and draw off the vital force. Some involve apparent supernatural elements, which have nothing to do with a desire to be a vampire or emulate a literary model of a vampire. But the characteristics of the experiences bear a striking resemblance to the vampire attacks described in early Eastern European accounts.

Chapter Nine

Dream Vampires

THE NOCTURNAL LANDSCAPE IS AN EERIE ONE: THE UN-real becomes real, fantasy becomes fact, the ghostly becomes solid, the impossible becomes obtainable. Time is distorted, the laws of physics are vanquished. We become aliens in our own minds.

Vampires roam this landscape. They materialize into the dreams of those who summon them through their intense interest in waking life. They also come unbidden to the unprepared and unwary. In some cases, they have the power to influence and change life.

Dreaming Is Believing

Jackie [a pseudonym] is a thirty-five-year-old woman who lives in Wyoming. She works part-time in a medical field. In her spare time, she loves to read vampire novels and watch vampire movies. For the past eight years, she has worked in local theater, and was involved in a production of a play called *Dracula, the Musical*. Jackie wrote to me about her vampire dreams.

Of all the vampire novels Jackie has read, the Anne Rice books are her favorites, so much so that she has read them at least three times each. In those books, *Interview with the Vampire, The Vampire Lestat,* and *The Queen of the Damned,* the characters of Lestat, Louis, and Armand are her favorites. "Their ability to feel, care, hope, share, and love has drawn me, as a reader, into their novels," Jackie said. "A person can actually feel and fall in love with the Rice vampires. They do not change into bats or dwell on the demonic, and I like that. The Rice vampires never seem to leave me with bad dreams. I'm not afraid of these vampires."

Shortly after reading one of the Rice books, Jackie dreamed of the vampires Lestat, Louis, and Armand. It was a pleasant dream and, as is the case with many dreams, slipped away from memory as she began to rise to waking consciousness. Then something unusual happened.

"I remember trying to wake up but couldn't," Jackie said. "I felt as if someone was calling out my name, then the feeling of someone holding me, snuggling up to my neck. It felt like a tingling pressure on my right side, a peaceful sensation." When she woke up, Jackie had a painful, sore neck. She examined it but found no marks. The soreness lasted about four days. "The only explanation is that I want to believe in the Rice vampires so much that I actually bring them into my dreams," she said.

"Not all my dreams about vampires are good," she went on. "I was glancing through a book called *Blood Lust*. It seemed to go more into the demonic part of a vampire. That night I had a nightmare that left me sweaty, nervous, and scared to go back to sleep. Another night I dreamed I was explaining the situation to my boyfriend and I barely touched the book, and again I woke up scared. I don't know what about this book bothers me, but I haven't picked it up since then!"

Jackie's vampire dreams seem to be triggered by what Freud termed "day residues," pieces of our waking life that filter into our dream life. But can vampire beings come into our dreams from some otherworldly place?

A Nocturnal Invitation

Vampires have visited the dreams of Karen Sue Powell-Chapman since she was twelve years old. They come bearing gifts of friendship and a feeling of protection.

Powell-Chapman is now in her early twenties and lives with her husband, Pat, in Lexington, Kentucky. She is sensitive, imaginative, and highly creative—she paints, draws, designs clothes and jewelry, and writes. For some of her writings, she uses the pseudonym of Selene Tempest—Selene being the Roman goddess of the moon. In addition, Powell-Chapman has something that sets her apart from most other people: She has the ability to dream lucidly and to control her dreams.

A lucid dream occurs when the dreamer is aware

that he or she is dreaming. Nearly everyone has at least one lucid dream during the course of a lifetime, but very few people have lucid dreams frequently. Knowledge of lucid dreams has existed since ancient times. Aristotle made mention of them in the fourth century BC, and the early Tibetan yogis valued them as part of their mystical development. The earliest existing written Western account of a lucid dream was penned in AD 415 by St. Augustine, who described the lucid dream of another man for the benefit of a physician.

There was little scientific interest in lucid dreaming until the 1960s. Since then, studies have been undertaken, but results have been inconsistent. Conclusions differ about the nature of lucid dreams and the ability of the individual to control them. However, scientists do agree that there are varying degrees of lucidity in dreams. In some cases, the dreamer may merely be aware of the dream and have no control over its outcome, while in other cases she may be able to direct the course of dream events to personal satisfaction. Scientists also agree that lucid dreams have some general characteristics: light (sometimes very bright), intense emotions, heightened colors and images, flying or levitation, and a sense of liberation or exhilaration.

Some researchers believe that lucid dreaming can enhance creativity and well-being in waking life, and that with training people can learn to have and control lucid dreams. However, experiments to induce and control dreams also have had inconsistent results. Other researchers are skeptical that dreams can be controlled on demand, despite the fact that Tibetan yogis have practiced dream control since at least the eighth century.

Powell-Chapman is a dream researcher's dream. Not only does she have lucid dreams, she has them nearly every night, programs them in advance, and influences their outcomes. Her dreams have all the general characteristics of lucid dreams. And whenever the moon is near full and full, her dreams intensify for several nights. Powell-Chapman's dream life has been that way as long as she can remember. In fact, she was startled when she learned that other people don't dream the same way.

As a child, Powell-Chapman had several favorite dream adventures. She would decide which one to take prior to falling asleep. In her dream, she would travel down a river that branched into two streams. She would choose one, and that branch would branch into two, and so on down the river. Each branch led to a different realm. In particular she liked to visit "Gem World," where a drinking fountain made of gems spouted different kinds of juices when the stones were pressed: grape juice from sapphires, strawberry juice from rubies, and so on. Another realm was "Meanville," characterized by dead trees and mean people. Powell-Chapman would always attempt to make the residents of Meanville happy. If she did so, a green patch would appear and the nearest trees would start growing again.

When Powell-Chapman was twelve, a vampire appeared in her dreams. He came unbidden, a tall, handsome, dark-haired man dressed in black. He appeared to be in his twenties. He had no fangs nor anything about his appearance that suggested "vampire." Yet somehow Powell-Chapman knew that was what he was. The dream initiated a series of dream encounters between Powell-Chapman and a group of vampires that has continued for more than a decade. The encounters seem to be leading toward a purpose.

Powell-Chapman keeps a dream diary. She graciously shared several entries relating to the vampires with me. Here is her account of her first vampire dream in November 1979:

The dream came around early November. The nights were dark and long. Moving from Frankfort to Lexington was hard for me at the age of twelve. We were already six weeks into the school year. I guess my parents didn't want to say anything about moving until they were sure they had the house in Lex. Everyone in school had already created their "cliques," so it made it that much harder to fit in. Our house was robbed twice before we got completely moved to Lexington. This only increased my feelings of insecurity.

Strange things happened in that house before the dream and got much stronger after it. I was having a hard time coping with all the normal changes. I didn't need the strange happenings. For example, when we moved into the house, my mom decided that my cat would stay out at night. I'd had the cat since I was eight years old, and it had always slept with me. Without the cat, I had problems sleeping.

One night I thought Mom had changed her mind because I felt something jump on the bed and pad around the room like my cat. I was able to sleep then and didn't think much of it. After a week went by, I reached down to pet my cat. There was nothing there but an indentation on the bed. I felt the bed rise below my hand and heard something pad out of the room. This frightened me. "It" didn't mimic my cat after that. I couldn't stand it anymore. I wasn't sure at first if it was my imagination or something else. Of course, later that became very clear.

The unusual events got stranger after the dream and I went to my father for help, but he had no idea as to what to do. I eventually, out of desperation, got around to asking our pastor. That was embarrassing enough in itself. He gave me a few ideas of what to do. I followed his instructions. This only seemed to anger it, whatever it was. So he told me to do something that was a little stronger. It became even more obvious that I was going to have to learn how to deal with it myself, and the same was true about other situations that came about later. I don't even know if the dream has any connection with the strange happenings or not.

The dream began with me looking down on two large yards connected by shrubs. Then I entered the first of the two yards. An opening was cut in the center of each of the farthest or back rows of shrubs in both yards for people to pass through. The back row of shrubs in the second yard was too tall to see over, but all the rest of the shrubs were trimmed slightly above waist-high. These two yards were full of students.

I had been going to school long enough at this point to recognize that the students were entirely from the new school that I was currently attending. I walked alone, unnoticed. The majority of the student body was in the first yard. They seemed to be having a party. There were some formed in groups. Most of them went from group to group. Groups merged and separated. They all seemed to be having fun. I watched for a while, and then was approached by a young man wearing all black.

When I first saw him, I knew that he was a vampire. He didn't say or do anything to suggest it—I just knew it. When he came up to me, we started talking. I did not recognize him, but I talked to him like we were longtime friends. As we talked, we moved toward the second yard. I don't remember what was said at this point. We passed through the opening in the hedge between the first and second yards. The opening was just large enough for us to pass through together comfortably.

The more flamboyant and popular students were in the second yard. They seemed quieter and kept to their groups. Here he pointed to several of the students and said that they could have had what he was offering me, but that they could not comprehend even the idea that he represented. I don't remember what was said, but we continued talking. We reached the end of the second yard. The opening in the tall hedges was before us and he asked if I was ready to proceed. I wasn't sure what he meant by this—whether it was a continuation of the dream or something more.

There was only enough room in this opening for one person to go through at a time. He half bowed and extended his arm toward the opening, offering for me to go first. I looked into the opening and could see nothing but darkness. When I stepped through, I woke from the dream.

I was sitting up in my bed looking into my dark room. A little light was provided by the picture window to the right of my bed. Then I noticed that at the end of the bed stood a dark figure. I will always clearly remember what he said to me then: "I will come back when you are ready."

I am positive that I was awake. I do not know of any way to test whether I was really awake then or not. All I can say is that I must trust what I believe to be true. The next night I don't remember any dreams, but my parents said that I slept walked [sic] into their room, said something, and then walked back to my room. They told me what I said and I would rather not disclose this information. To them it didn't mean anything, but to me it does. The next week or so after that they said that they heard weird noises coming from my room and saw flashing lights. They asked me what I had been doing. I am a light sleeper and have unusually good hearing, but I heard and saw nothing. All I could remember was feeling very rested. However, I seem to have developed some insomnia since.

Powell-Chapman felt comforted by the vampire. He seemed to be almost a guardian angel, looking out for her, telling her she was special, letting her know that in the midst of her insecurities in the new school, things were all right. She shared her dream with a few of her friends at school. They in turn told others. Some students asked her to tell the dream, and for a short time she was the center of attention. Others thought the dream was exciting; one person seemed frightened of Powell-Chapman after hearing it. The following Halloween, Powell-Chapman dressed up as a vampire. Some of the kids nicknamed her "Vampire."

The dream opened Powell-Chapman's interest in the occult. She began to learn more about psychic phenomena and vampires. But no more vampire dreams occurred for about a year. Then the vampire dreams began to occur about once or twice a year until Powell-Chapman was eighteen, when they increased in frequency to four or five times a year. They increased in frequency again when she turned twenty-one. Meanwhile, she discovered she had a natural gift for psychometry, which is the psychic reading of objects by holding them and intuiting information about the people who have owned or handled them. She also had a natural gift for clairvoyance and precognition, the ability to see beyond the immediate environment and the ability to see into the future, respectively. For a time when she was twenty, she lived in a haunted house with her brother, Scott, and a friend. The house was haunted by three apparitions who visited her from time to time and could be seen at night.

Strangely, when it came to the vampires, Powell-Chapman found her control over the dreams to be limited. She could manipulate other people and things, but not the vampires themselves. Nor could she summon them the way she could create other dreams.

After the appearance of the first vampire, other

vampires began appearing as minor players in larger dream dramas. For example, Powell-Chapman would enter a house and find in it individuals, male and female, who were vampires. Again, there was nothing obviously vampiric about their appearance or behavior; she just "knew" they were vampires.

Gradually, the vampires revealed why they were appearing in her dreams. One reason was that they wished to dispel the stereotypes presented by books and movies. They aren't all dark-haired; some are blond or brunette. They eat food like humans. They enjoy wine.

"They allow me to see how they act in daily routines," Powell-Chapman told me. "Some want to be eccentric and mysterious, and others want to lead as normal an existence as possible. They don't necessarily all live in dark castles with damp walls. They often choose to live in groups in a house rather than be alone, because they are so different that limiting interaction to only the normal world would cause problems. They have the ability to feel what other people are feeling. It can damage them if they come in contact with someone who is very angry."

In introducing Powell-Chapman to their lifestyle, the vampires did not show themselves drinking blood. In later dreams they talked about it, but not as a necessity for survival. Blood-drinking among them is ritualistic and symbolic, and is used as a sign of recognition.

Another purpose the vampires have revealed is to invite Powell-Chapman to become initiated into their ranks. In March 1989 she had a dream that took place in a New England–type of town on the coast. She encountered four local youths, three boys and a girl, who exhibited threatening behavior toward her. She realized they could do her no harm because she was a vampire. This realization shocked her. She showed no fear toward the youths, and they became bored and left. Powell-Chapman flew about for a while, and then caught sight of a man in black who glided through the crowd of people. He seemed to be associated with the vampire figure who had first appeared in her dreams at age twelve.

In the dream, said Powell-Chapman, "he stopped and looked up. We looked at each other. His essence seemed to possess me. I sensed it invading the very depths of my soul. He saw into mine and I saw into his. It felt like a reflection of myself. When he had drawn back into himself, I knew he wanted me to follow." This she did, and eventually found him standing at the ocean's edge with the water lapping near his feet. Powell-Chapman experienced a feeling of great tranquility. "I stood awhile enjoying the comfort of his presence," she said. "I had the feeling he would be there when I needed him. Perhaps this was the message I had been searching for throughout the dream. I experienced complete contentment."

But her status as a dream vampire seemed to be the expression of wish or expectation, for subsequent dreams returned her to the status of vampire-in-training.

In May 1989, she dreamed of meeting a dark male who greeted her as an old friend. He told her of the existence of "supersapiens," a secret race of beings, apparently vampires, that had existed for centuries. The race existed on both the astral and physical levels.

The man told her that his race had "an unusual thirst that can only be satisfied with blood, even though it is not necessary for survival."

Occasionally, human beings cross the line between the races and become one of the supersapiens, he said. Such candidates are born with the possibility, and if they choose to take advantage of it, are then given dream assignments to prepare them for the change-over. Powell-Chapman understood that she was a candidate. She felt elated when she awoke.

In March 1990, she dreamed of being heir to the "vampire legacy" as a protégée of a female vampire. As an indication of her sincere desire to be taken as a protégée, Powell-Chapman cut a finger and put a few drops of her own blood in a glass of wine. The vampire drank the wine, then took Powell-Chapman's arm, bit into it, and began to drink her blood.

The vampire told her that one bite would not turn her into a vampire. After two bites, Powell-Chapman would become like one of the vampire's servants. She would have to struggle to retain her own will. She would experience, to a modest degree, some of the vampires' supernormal abilities. Upon the third bite, Powell-Chapman would be an immortal vampire.

This female vampire then told her that prior to the third bite, she had to ritualistically take a life. The vampire asked her if she was prepared to accept the vampire legacy. Powell-Chapman replied yes and offered her neck. The vampire bit into her jugular vein.

In a subsequent dream, Powell-Chapman found herself in a society of vampires, whom she described in her dream journal as "happy, friendly, and successful." She was now like them, and was invited to join their ranks. The vampires flew about in the air and were "appealing and childlike in their purity." Powell-Chapman discovered that she could fly, too. When faced with a dark and threatening vampire, she flew away.

I asked if her vampire dreams had brought any changes in her. "Yes," she answered. "My mind seems clearer and I tend to worry less. I've had more confidence and seem to be able to relate to people better. I can make more eye contact. I used to be shy. I wasn't happy because I felt alone a lot. A lot of my activities were TV shows or books. I kept to myself. Now I love to go out and do things, get my own projects working and include other people in them."

In addition, Powell-Chapman seems to be in harmony with the flow of energies and forces around her. Others are drawn to her and seem to want to do things for her. "Strangers have begun to strike up conversations, even if it was out of their way to start them," she said. "Waiters or waitresses tend to give me free meals or extras and such. I sometimes know what people are thinking. It used to happen with friends or family, but now it is more frequent and spontaneous and can be with strangers as well. Events seem to happen the way I need them to occur. For example, when I *need* money, something happens so that I will have it. It has to be a need, though, not a want. I do feel like something is taking care of me, watching over me."

Do Powell-Chapman's dream vampires exist on

their own in another reality, or are they constructs from her own unconscious, formed to help bring information to the surface? A psychologist would argue for the latter. In dream analysis, the psyche is understood to speak to the dreamer in the dreamer's own language, by using symbols familiar to the dreamer. Thus, a farmer dreams in a farm milieu and a computer programmer dreams in a computer milieu.

In the psychology of the great Carl G. Jung, dream symbols take on shape from the dreamer's personal unconscious—the reservoir of forgotten or repressed memories—as well as from the collective unconscious, the deep reservoir of memories shared collectively by the human race. This collective reservoir contains all the impressions and impulses since the beginning of human history. Thus, a vampire in a dream expresses whatever attributes and qualities have been endowed it by accumulated collective thought, and by an individual's own beliefs and perceptions. In Powell-Chapman's case, it could be said that the vampire is a symbol representing a specialness and uniqueness, someone to be both respected and feared. Her dream induction into this elite status may be the psyche's way of improving self-confidence in waking life.

However, too little is known about dreams and consciousness to relegate dream images strictly to an interior landscape. In a human being, where does "consciousness" reside and what are its bounds? What exactly are dreams, and do they touch other realities beyond the physical plane? Science does not know.

Nor can it be said for certain what is "real" in an alternate reality. The kaleidoscope shifts again.

Powell-Chapman has come to see the vampire dreams as astral visitations. "I enjoy having the visits," she said. "I think it would be neat if I saw one of these vampire people in real life."

Chapter Ten

A Night in Dracula's Castle

THE RUINED CASTLE OF VLAD TEPES, KNOWN POPULARLY as "Castle Dracula," sits high on a mountain rock overlooking the source of the Arges River in what is now Romania. In Tepes's day, the sovereign land was known as Wallachia. The original castle was not built by Tepes, but was in ruins by the time he came across it in the fifteenth century. Called Poenari, the castle probably was built in the fourteenth century. Compared to other castles, it was small and narrow, about 100 feet wide by 120 feet long. Perched on a remote peak north of the city of Curtea-de-Arges, it nonetheless had strategic importance because of its location near the Hungarian border, and probably served as an early-warning lookout post for Castle Bran, a much larger castle on the other side of the mountains.

The castle had been devastated by the past attacks of invading Turks and Tatars. After he seized power in

Wallachia in 1456, Tepes looked around for an ideal fortress and found it in the ruins of Poenari. He had it rebuilt by enslaving the boyar class.

In Wallachia, there were two main classes of society: the peasants and the boyars. The boyars were a native aristocracy, some of whom were landowners and others of whom were tenants. Many were distinguished military officers. They had dominion over large estates that included entire villages, and ruled the peasant populations therein as feudal lords. The collective power of the boyars posed a threat to Tepes. Many of the boyars wanted to appease the hostile Turks on the other side of the border. Tepes set about to break the boyar class by creating a military loyal only to him and not to various boyars, and by turning the boyars into peasant slaves.

In 1457, Tepes, aided by a loyal military force, began a systematic campaign to rid the land of his enemies and potential enemies. On Easter Day, he rounded up a large number of boyars and their wives and children. Many were immediately impaled on stakes. Others were manacled and chained and marched off to Poenari in their Easter finery, where they were forced to labor to rebuild the ruined castle. The peasants at Poenari surely must have been mystified to see the upper class turned into a chain gang, building brick and lime kilns, hauling stones up the steep mountainside, and laying bricks to rebuild the castle walls. Each trip up required at least an hour to reach the castle. For months the boyars toiled, whipped until their clothing fell off in shreds. Untold numbers perished from beatings, starvation, dehydration, and exhaustion, and from falling down the mountain. This spectacular subjugation of a powerful class established Tepes's reputation for extreme cruelty.

Once restored, the castle seemed to be virtually impregnable. From its five towers, soldiers would be able to catch attackers in crossfire. Its extra-thick walls of stone reinforced with brick were built to withstand cannon fire. Legend has it that, as a final precaution, Tepes also had constructed a secret escape passage leading from the castle's well through the mountain and into a cave on the banks of the Arges River.

Despite his fortress, Tepes was eventually defeated by the dreaded Turks, who successfully besieged him at Poenari in 1462. In despair, Tepes's wife committed suicide by flinging herself off a tower balcony into the river. Tepes, more coolheaded, is said to have escaped via his secret route. He eventually returned to power, but in 1476 he was killed, probably by an assassin. Legend has it that his corpse was beheaded and mutilated and tossed in a marsh near the monastery of Snagov. Monks allegedly found the remains and secretly buried them in a crypt. But excavations in 1931 revealed no casket, only a hole with animal bones in it.

After Tepes abandoned Castle Poenari, it once again fell victim to ravages by the Turks, who partially dismantled it. The castle was not occupied at all by Tepes's successor, Radu the Handsome. It was used by Tepes's only legitimate son by his second wife, but then was abandoned again for good. Power shifted away toward Bucharest; the castle was no longer of value. Decay set in. By the turn of the twentieth century, it was a mass of crumbling brick and stone covered with vines and brush. Some of the structure had fallen away into the river. In 1940, a massive earthquake further reduced it.

The exact location of Tepes's castle was unknown until the 1960s, when two scholars found it. Raymond T. McNally and Radu R. Florescu, who had researched the life of Tepes as the historical role model for Stoker's Count Dracula, succeeded in identifying the remains as those that had once housed the infamous Wallachian prince. Thanks largely to tourist interest, the Romanian government then allocated funds for restoration work.

As was noted in Chapter Three, Tepes is popularly thought to be a vampire (a view greeted with amusement by Romanians), probably because of Stoker's use of him as a historical model for Count Dracula. Florescu and McNally have said that they discovered a document alleging that on at least one occasion Tepes drank the blood of his impaled victims. However, the practice of victors drinking the blood of the conquered is a symbolic act of complete victory. It is a universal practice almost pre-dating history and has nothing to do with vampirism in a supernatural sense. There is no evidence to indicate that Tepes otherwise had a desire or need for blood.

Even though Tepes was not a vampire, the castle has long had a reputation of exuding an atmosphere of evil. In 1977, Vincent Hillyer, an American adventurer, gained the rare permission to spend a night alone in Dracula's castle. Mysterious and unsettling things happened, including puncture wounds on Hillyer's neck. Since then, Hillyer has devoted time to researching, writing on, and speaking about vampires and the supernatural. His book *Vampires* was published in 1988. With the publisher, Loose Change

Publications, Hillyer is offering a reward of $10,000 in gold bullion "to anyone who can bring in a resurrected corpse in the human vampire state." To date there have been no takers. (In case there are any readers who think they have the proper goods, please note that Loose Change specifies no night deliveries.)

A dapper man with continental flair, Hillyer has spent a good portion of his life jet-setting about the globe in stellar company. In the 1950s, he was married to the Shah of Iran's younger sister, Fatemeh, and lived in the royal household. He has explored the jungles of Borneo, worked as an actor in Rome, owned airline and export agencies in Teheran and Beverly Hills, lived at the Ritz-Carlton in Paris, participated in psychical research experiments, and investigated haunted houses in California. Presently, he lives in Los Banos, California.

We had the opportunity to meet when he paid a visit to New York City. What better meeting place than the Count Dracula Fan Club museum, where, with President Jeanne Youngson, we settled in amidst the comfortable clutter of bats, books, and other vampire paraphernalia.

"I've been interested in vampires since I was a child and first saw Bela Lugosi in *Dracula,* followed by *The Mark of the Vampire* with Lionel Barrymore a few years later," Hillyer said. "I was always reading stories and comic books with a vampire theme. I just felt an attraction to the subject. It always was interesting, it was fun, it was diverting and anything but boring. Later, when I was in college, I met a very interesting man, the psychical researcher Dr. Hereward Carrington. I assisted him in some of his experiments on mental telepathy and psychokinesis."

"Do you have exceptional psychic ability?" I asked.

Hillyer shook his head. "No more than the average person. I mean, everybody gets a little hunch or premonition. Anyway, Dr. Carrington told me of various vampire incidents, and that increased my interest in vampires."

Hillyer's first encounters with the beliefs in supernatural beings took place during his years as the shah's brother-in-law. He was even taken for a vampire by superstitious villagers.

"We were living in a very old palace in Teheran called Sahab Garanieh Palace," Hillyer recounted. "It was an edifice about 300 years old. One of the eighteenth-century shahs, Nasr-i-Din, had lived there and reputedly still haunted this palace. We lived on the upper floor in one wing. It was too difficult to try to heat the whole palace—we only had small fireplaces in each room. We had nine servants, and they were all deathly afraid to go down to the subterranean rooms below where the old shah had maintained a favorite chamber. There once was a pool there, the ruins of which were still in the room. The old shah would sit on a big cushion there with his dozens of wives and concubines around him.

"Even though our servants didn't want to go downstairs, there were times when they *had* to go down to find things that had been stored. I decided I would take them down myself and show them that there was nothing to be afraid of. One windy evening, we all got candles and lighted them, and went down. I did want to dispel their fears, of course, but I was half hoping at the same time that maybe there really *was* something that they should be fearful of. There I was, leading this group of very timorous people, and from nowhere a sudden shift of wind came up and blew out all the candles. I heard a commotion behind me, and by the time I got my candle lit, I was alone. The servants had taken off and run back upstairs. The wind was eerie and was making strange sounds in these lower chambers. I always wondered about that wind and the way and moment it came up. None of the servants would ever go back down there again. Nothing I could do could convince them to go. Maybe the old shah *was* haunting the place."

Hillyer offered another story about the local beliefs in the supernatural. "Out in the villages there were beliefs that some people could change into spirits. They didn't necessarily call them vampires, they called them *djinn* or *afrit,* which are demons in Arabian mythology. The villagers were very superstitious. I went to a village up north one time, in the province of Mazanderan on the Caspian Sea, and I sat having tea on a large carpet near a stream with the chief. Through an interpreter, he told me about a man in the village who used to go out hunting tigers armed only with an axe. People don't realize that northern Iran is all jungle, filled with tigers and wild pigs. The tigers are the large Persian tiger, second in size only to the Bengal tiger of India.

"The chief said that one day the hunter went out and followed a tiger. Unbeknownst to him, a second tiger was following *him.* He never came back. The people believed that he had been turned into a weretiger.

"Once I made a trip on horseback with some of the shah's brothers, and we went through a village called Kelardasht in the Alborz Mountains. It was late afternoon, and the people were all standing in the little dirt streets. As we passed by, the men turned away and the women put part of their veils up higher over their eyes. I wondered what had happened— 'Did I forget to shower this morning?'—because everyone was shunning me. I asked one of the guides with us, and he said, 'You have blue eyes, and the people here believe that blue eyes belong only to a demon. They are afraid of you, and they're afraid you can transform yourself into some type of creature and drink their blood.' That night, when I went out walking through the streets, even the dogs ran off. I felt safer than I would on the streets of New York— nobody came near me! It gave me a funny feeling.

"Then I met a very interesting Englishman who came to Iran on an exchange program to teach English at some of the schools there. He had brilliant red hair, a red mustache and beard. Turned out he was an English Witch. I thought that was interesting, in light of the widespread superstition that people with red hair are Witches. One evening he talked to me about various incantations and spells that he used, and said that the same methods were used in Iran, such as tying knots in a string, or sending orange seeds in a letter.

"Fatemeh told me that the Queen Mother sometimes used witchcraft against Fatemeh's own mother, because they were both wives of the old shah. He had four wives and various children came from the wives. The Queen Mother would send her servants out every morning to check her front doorstep to make sure there were no black roosters slain and put there to curse her. A lot of this sort of witchcraft and magic goes on in Iran."

Around 1974, Hillyer met scholars Raymond T. McNally and Radu Florescu, who have made a publishing profession out of researching Vlad Tepes as the historical model for Count Dracula. From them, Hillyer learned of the discovery of the ruins of Castle Dracula, and knew immediately that he had to see it for himself.

But securing permission to stay overnight alone in the ruins was another matter. The Romanian government turned Hillyer down. Several years passed. Then Fatemeh, who by then was divorced from Hillyer, pulled some diplomatic strings for him and got him the coveted permission.

Hillyer journeyed to Romania in 1977. In Bucharest, he met with Deputy Minister of Tourism H. E. Stefan Enache, who tried to dissuade him from staying alone in the castle during the night. It was too dangerous, Enache said, but not because of vampires—a superstition not officially tolerated by the Communist regime—but because of bears, wolves, and other creatures. The ruins offered no protection against the very real beasts of the night. Just prior to Hillyer's arrival, a German hiker walking in the Arges Valley near the castle had been torn to pieces by a bear. Furthermore, local laws prohibited Hillyer from carrying a weapon.

Hillyer would not be swayed, and so Enache dispatched him with a guide, Michaela Velescu. Velescu took him on a week-long trip through Transylvania, culminating in their arrival at the foot of the Carpathian ridge where the ruined castle sits. There Hillyer was left by his guide. It was late in the afternoon, and the ruins looked forbidding in the gathering shadows. "When I saw it in the dying rays of the sun, I felt this thrill," he recalled. "It was the culmination of a dream. Here was the castle of the man, or creature, or whatever you're going to term this legendary character—this was his lair, and I was going to enter it, spend the night, hoping against hope that he might just show up with a benevolent gesture to welcome me or something like that."

Hillyer picked up his bundle, consisting of a blanket roll, lantern, and bag containing dinner, and began the slow climb up the steep 1,531 steps leading to the castle. As he mounted the steps, he thought about the threat of bears. "I had no weapon of any kind, other than a cross," he said. "And I thought, That's not going to scare the bears away. I'm a state humane officer in California, so I thought if worse came to worst, I could always hit him with this large cheese and a bottle of wine I was carrying in my provisions. Or threaten him with a citation!"

"Did you wear the cross as protection against vampires?" I asked.

Hillyer shrugged. "Why not? Better to be safe than sorry. I put it in my pocket. I didn't tell the Romanian authorities because of the Communist position on religion. I suppose if I'd had a pizza, it probably would have been just as effective—all that garlic!"

He resumed his story. "It took me about an hour and a half to climb the steps. When I got to the top, it was just about sunset. The wind had come up, and it was a cold, biting wind, even though it was the month of July. My leather jacket was soaked through from the perspiration of all that climbing, and I felt quite a chill.

"The first thing I did when I went inside was to check the different rooms and the little narrow stairs going upstairs to orient myself so I wouldn't walk around in the darkness and go in the wrong place or fall somewhere.

"When the sun did set, I sat down in what would have been the main hallway. The roof was all broken in this old castle, so it was exposed to the night sky and the elements. I set out the provisions I'd brought for dinner—a smoked ham, a sharp white cheese, bread, some fresh vine-ripened tomatoes, and a bottle of vintage red wine. After that long climb, I was hungry and the food tasted wonderful. I'd noticed all these little pebbles on the floor around me. Suddenly all the little 'pebbles' started jumping around and moving! I held up my lantern, and saw that they were fat, scaly, shiny beetles and ugly, hairy, *huge* spiders. They were crawling all over, coming up my pant leg. They looked ferocious. The beetles were varying sizes, anywhere from the size of a ten-cent piece up to the size of a twenty-five-cent piece. The spiders were of myriad sizes and shapes. They all seemed to move so fast in my direction. I frantically brushed them off, and got rid of them by setting out some of my food for them. And they were *ravenous*. Really greedy! They crawled all over the food, eating.

"I moved farther down the hallway to avoid being overrun by them and to await the approaching night. I could hear the chirping of birds and bats. Soon I heard the wolves begin to howl, and that was delightful, because then it really set the scene. Here we have a film in the making: The wolves are starting to howl as night descends and darkness covers everything.

"I reminded myself of what the Romanian officials had told me about the bears and wolves coming into the castle at night on some occasions—neither of which are known to be overly friendly to visitors. So I determined that if they came, I would go up a little narrow stairway to this room at the top of the tower. It was a small opening and I could block it with some of the loose stones lying around. Or I could stand there and shout—you know, scare the animals a little bit if they began to act unfriendly.

"This little room might have been the room that Dracula's first wife had jumped from when she committed suicide. There is one spot where the natives say her blood still colors the Arges River. In actuality, the red color to the water probably comes from the red sandstone in the area.

"That night, when I looked down, I could see the moonlight reflecting on the river, and I thought about the dramatic events that happened here. Dracula escaped through a secret tunnel. The cad didn't take his wife with him.

"Then I heard these noises downstairs. I thought, 'Oh, boy, I wonder if the animals have come in.' I peeked down the stairs, but I didn't see anything. It was a little hazardous to try to sleep in this upstairs room, so I went back down the hall and put out my blanket and went to sleep. I was so tired, and I wasn't afraid to sleep. I fell into a heavy, uncomfortable sleep and had this strange dream that I was riding in a horse-drawn carriage that was rushing pell-mell up a winding mountain pass with precipitous cliffs. I seemed to be pursuing someone. The carriage shot around a sharp corner and came suddenly upon a Gypsy woman who was beating a fallen horse. The horse was dead, and its eyes stared blankly at the heavens. I was angered at the Gypsy's cruelty, and I shouted at her that I would never invite her into my house.

"I came awake with an ominous sense of a presence, like somebody, or something, was watching me. Then I noticed this pain at my collarbone and rubbed it. I was shocked to see little drops of blood on my finger. I immediately thought, Nobody is going to believe this, I spent the night in Dracula's castle and got puncture wounds! But I didn't have time to think about the wounds because of this overpowering feeling that I was not alone, that somebody was watching me. And it was so strong that it made me turn and look down to the end of the hallway. I had to decide whether to go down and investigate or stay there safely under the blanket and forget the whole thing.

"I decided to investigate. I walked down to the end of the hall half expecting to meet Dracula himself. I saw these watery, glassy eyes in the darkness. But it was an old wolf. I assumed it was old because it had a gray muzzle and backed off fast and ran down the mountainside.

"As the wolf retreated, I noticed a powerful odor of rotting flowers spreading through the chamber. I was puzzled because I had observed earlier that there were no flowers around the ruins at all. I knew I wasn't going back to sleep, and I was chilled to the bone from the wind blowing through the place. It was near sunrise, and I decided to leave, even though it was still dark. But I felt in a bit of a jocose mood, so I went back upstairs on the balcony and I waved my lantern and howled like a Transylvanian miscreant. Way off in the distance I could see the fire of a Gypsy camp, and I thought my voice just might carry—at least they could see this lamp swinging back and forth.

"Then I started back down. Even though the sun rose, the light still didn't penetrate the thick forest, and I had to make my way through the darkness with my lantern. I panicked when I heard twigs break behind me, and I knew I was being followed. I thought maybe this time a wolf wouldn't be frightened off so easily. I began to walk faster, but whatever it was behind me was coming up fast. Below me I saw a light—a flashlight perhaps—and I shouted. There was a shrill whistle and I heard a thundering of paws behind me. I thought I surely would be attacked, but the paws raced past me. They were two hunting dogs, evidently answering their master's signal.

"Once I reached the valley, I had to walk several miles before I came upon a power station with a telephone. I called the Posada Inn, where my guide and driver were staying. The driver came to pick me up. When I walked into the Posada Inn, Mrs. Velescu and the mayor of Curtea were startled at my appearance. I had a cold sweat. I went to lift my arms, and I just felt so rotten, so nauseated. I must have looked great, just coming in from Dracula's castle—pallid, about ready to faint, and with a bloody neck. They took me right away to the Curtea-de-Arges hospital. Mrs. Velescu didn't believe that I had been bitten. She was startled when the doctor told her I had puncture wounds.

"The doctor seemed divided between whether he should be concerned or amused at my predicament, having been bitten at Dracula's castle. He kept saying, 'No, no, it wasn't Dracula, it wasn't Dracula, it was a spider.' It must have been a very big spider, because there was about a half an inch between the two wounds. He gave me an antitoxin shot, but I was sick with nausea, fever, and malaise for about twenty-four hours. The bite healed in a few days. I was just hoping it would leave some scars, because I knew my friends were going to find it hard to believe. When I've given lectures and mentioned the doctor's diagnosis of the bite of a large spider, I've had a number of people in the audience say, 'How do you know that wasn't Dracula?' I don't say it, I let the audience say it.

"After I returned to the States, I went to see a dermatologist because I kept getting sunburned so badly, and I would get dry areas on the skin called keratoses that are a pre-skin-cancer condition caused by severe sunburn. They have to be burned off with frozen nitrogen. The doctor told me I was very sensitive to the sun and would have to wear sunscreen or a hat. I was surprised because I'd never had this trouble before. He said, 'Well, you do now.'

"I told him about the incident in the castle, and he said, 'That's very interesting. But it still boils down to the fact that you're sensitive to the sun, whatever the cause is, or whatever you *think* the cause is.' The mind can do strange things. I'm still sensitive to the sun more than thirteen years later. I go out with a hat. I stay out of the direct sunlight. Even in a car, I have to put a shade down on the side, or I will be burnt red."

Hillyer related his experience to experts, among them Professor Corneliu Barbulescu of the Romanic Folkloric Institute in Bucharest, Florescu, McNally, Dr. Devandra Varma—a vampirologist from India— and several psychical researchers in southern California. From them, Hillyer pieced together theories about what had happened to him at Dracula's castle. The castle itself may be a sort of psychic magnet for evil because of its bloody history and the huge number of corpses buried on the mountaintop. The dream of not inviting the Gypsy woman in could relate to the superstition that the vampire cannot enter a house unless it first has been invited in. And the smell of rotting flowers might have signaled the presence of malevolent forces. Smells are common in hauntings and possession cases—the worse the smell, the more negative the presence. Hillyer is open-minded but noncommittal about these explanations.

"You received a lot of media publicity when you came back to the States," I said. "How did others react to your story?"

"Some with disbelief, and some seemed to confirm their own theories about vampires," Hillyer said. "Others were unsure what to think. My friends all knew I was sincere."

"Do you believe in vampires?"

"I can't deny that they exist, because who can say, really, one way or the other? It's easy to scoff at something. Like old Bill Shakespeare was fond of saying, 'there are more things in heaven and earth.' I always have felt that when people talk about and believe in something long enough, there is a basis for that belief. However, I don't see how a corpse could dematerialize and then rematerialize physically outside the grave—that strains credulity. But it's very possible that the astral body is the actual vampire, projecting out from the corpse, feeding on the living and returning to the corpse to sustain it."

Hillyer has developed a theory called the "hemolytic factor" to explain how an astral form can draw off the blood of a living person. The theory rests on the process of hemolysis, which is the destruction of red corpuscles by hemolysin, a substance in the blood serum, that occurs with the release of hemoglobin into surrounding fluids. This effect is sometimes produced when red corpuscles from a different blood group are injected into the blood.

According to the hemolytic factor theory, the vampire's astral body penetrates the victim's aura and physical body. The vampire, which is in great need of blood, has sparse red corpuscles and can be considered the "wrong blood group." Hemolysis occurs, and the vampire sucks up the red corpuscles released in the victim's blood. These are transported back to the grave and infused into the corpse.

Since publication of his book on vampires, Hillyer has had occasional bizarre or disturbing encounters with both those who like the subject and those who don't.

"One evening, the woman who owns the local bookstore in Los Banos, Phoenix Books, called me at home. She said, 'There's somebody here who came down from San Francisco to get a copy of your book, and now wants to meet you. A girl. I don't want to send her to your house because she looks a little odd, and I think it's better if you come down here.'

"So I went down to the store, and there was this girl who was about twenty-five years of age. There were two young men with her. All three were dressed entirely in black. The girl was wearing a cocktail dress, very decolleté front and back, with a black hat. She had on black lipstick and black fingernail polish. One fellow had his hair combed straight up in the air. Both fellows were wearing silver earrings and riding boots with silver spurs, and black shirts and pants. The girl said that they were vampires and belonged to a vampire group in San Francisco, and that the fellows were dressed like the men in the film *Near Dark*. She said she wanted to have a photo taken, if it was all right with me. One of the fellows had a camera. I said, 'You have everything, where's your pentagram?' She said, 'Here,' and pulled her dress down in the back to show me where she had a tattoo of a pentagram just below the shoulder. She stood close to me, and gave a little smile. She had canine teeth that were about a quarter of an inch longer than her other teeth. I looked closely, and they weren't plastic. She may have gone to a dentist and had permanent fangs capped in her mouth, or they may have been her own teeth, I don't know. But they were long. And sharp. And she was from San Francisco."

"Which may explain everything," I said dryly. "Did the photo come out?"

"I don't know," Hillyer said. "They never sent me one. But they left an address and said, 'We will be in touch with you, because we would like to have you come up to one of our group meetings sometime.' I said as nonchalantly as I could, 'I'll think about it.' After they left, a man customer who had been watching us said, 'Did you see those teeth? She could *bite*. I wouldn't go up there to San Francisco—she might bite you.' I thought it was good advice. A while later, Joanne, the owner of the bookstore, wrote to them at the address they'd given, and the letter came back marked that there was no such address. Very strange."

Hillyer said that trouble has come from religious groups who equate vampires with satanism. "There is a small group of religious fanatics who have been making life difficult for me from time to time. They go into the libraries and start burning or defacing my book. They threatened to burn down the funeral chapel and the city hall because the city proclaimed a holiday when my book came out—Vampire Day in Los Banos. Vampirism has nothing to do with satanism. The two are not remotely related. Movies and novels relate the two and people start believing it."

Hillyer decried the increasing commercialization of Dracula in Romania for the benefit of the tourist trade. It was taking place under the Communist government, and probably will accelerate now that the country has opened to the West. The lobby of Hotel Dracula in Cluj near the Borgo Pass contains coffins, and guests are invited to lie in them and have their pictures taken. Anything associated with Vlad Tepes, the "historical Dracula," however inaccurate that label might be, is grist for a tour itinerary. Even Tepes's birthplace in the village of Sighisoara has been turned into a restaurant.

"Can you imagine," mused Hillyer, "Dracula's mother raising a little kid like him: 'Dracula! Come back in. It's time to have dinner. We have blood sausage tonight!'"

Epilogue

Can we now answer the question "Do vampires exist?"

Yes. Vampires do exist because we believe in them. Vampires exist in subjective reality, the internal landscape of our consciousness. Vampires have the capability of existing in objective reality—the external world—when conditions are right. When Vampire Reality is created.

In earlier times, the belief that the dead return to plague the living was a powerful one, giving vampires an objective reality. "This was a peculiar kind of fear and awe, both fearing the dead and perhaps wanting them to come back," said Bernard Davies, cofounder and chairman of the Dracula Society in London. "Before the Reformation, the afterlife was regarded as a dark world of cold and deprivation, lacking all the things from this life. It was natural to think that those passing over would want to get back to the world of the living." If people had greater, natural mediumistic ability, as might have been likely in more primitive times, then the collective psychic thought concerning the dead "might have had an effect on those with whom one had strong links, to conjure up these vampiric manifestations," said Davies. "But the Reformation began to promote the idea that the afterlife was a blessed state. It gave the poor something to look forward to. People ceased to fear dying and began to glorify the afterlife. Once simple people grasped this idea, they ceased to fear the return of the dead. That killed the obsession on which vampirism could have fed."

Instead, the vampire entered Western literature, where it enjoyed new incarnations as a near-human being with a demonic, dark side. This subjective, glamorous vampire also can become objective reality when sufficiently powered by our beliefs. Vampires *are* among us, in a variety of guises. The vampire reveals itself to us as an unseen attacker, as a disembodied entity, as a mysterious person, as a shape in the shadows, as a figure in dreams. And when desire is strong enough to become a vampire, a genuine transformation occurs. Ultimately, the face we present to the world is the sum total of what we believe we are.

Appendix

Organizations and Publications

The following are some of the organizations and publications of interest to vampire aficionados. For the latest fees for memberships, subscriptions, and sample issues, send a letter with a self-addressed, stamped envelope to the appropriate person or organization. The self-addressed, stamped envelope is most important—most clubs and organizations operate on limited budgets. For overseas inquiries, send an International Reply Coupon, which can be obtained from the U.S. Postal Service.

UNITED STATES

Count Dracula Fan Club
Dr. Jeanne K. Youngson, president
29 Washington Square West, Penthouse North
New York, NY 10011

Founded in 1965, the club is geared to appeal to all age groups. Sends newsletters and journals, holds annual open house, maintains a Dracula Museum and more. For a sample copy of the journal and full membership information, send $4.00 U.S. to the address above.

Vampire Information Exchange
Eric S. Held, director
P.O. Box 328
Brooklyn, NY 11229-0328

Information clearinghouse. Publishes the *Vampire Information Exchange Newsletter* six times a year.

Appendix

Miss Lucy Westenra Society of the Undead
Lewis Sanders, president
125 Taylor St.
Jackson, TN 38301

Publishes three to four newsletters annually.

Count Dracula Society
Dr. Donald A. Reed, national president
334 West 54th St.
Los Angeles, CA 90037
(213) 752-5811

The Anne Rice's Vampire Lestat Fan Club
P.O. Box 58277
New Orleans, LA 70158-8277

Publishes a quarterly newsletter and offers a pen pal program.

The Collinsport Record, The Collinwood Journal, and *The Friends of "Dark Shadows"*
Sharida Rizzuto, editor
P.O. Box 213
Metrairie, LA 70004

"Dark Shadows" fan publications.

The Vampire Journal
Thomas Schellenberger, president
Sharida Rizzuto, editor and publisher
P.O. Box 994
Metrairie, LA 70004

Publishes quarterly journal and triannual newsletters.

Count Ken Fan Club
Ken Gilbert, president
18 Palmer St.
Salem, MA 01970

Publishes monthly newsletter.

Vampire Studies
Martin V. Riccardo, director
P.O. Box 151
Berwyn, IL 60402

Not a membership organization. Information clearinghouse, lectures. Interested in hearing about vampire fantasies.

Vampire Research Center
Stephen Kaplan, director
P.O. Box 252
Elmhurst, NY 11373

Information clearinghouse. Collects data on vampires.

UNITED KINGDOM

The Vampyre Society
Allen J. Gittens, founder and president
38 Westcroft
Chippenham
Wiltshire SN14 OLY
England

Publishes quarterly journal, *For the Blood Is the Life.*

International Society for the Advancement of Irreproducible Vampire and Lycanthropy Research
Rev. Sean Manchester, founder and president
P.O. Box 542
Highgate
London N6 6BG
England

Membership by invitation only. Publishes quarterly newsletter, *The Cross and the Stake.*

Vampire Reseach Society
Rev. Sean Manchester, founder and president
P.O. Box 542
Highgate
London N6 6BG
England

For a deluxe hardcover copy of *The Highgate Vampire*, completely revised and expanded, 1991, by The Right Rev. Sean Manchester, O.S.G., send a check or international money order for £25.00 made payable to the Vampire Research Society at the above address. Payment *must* be made in pounds sterling. Amount covers postage and handling.

The Dracula Society
Bernard Davies, honorable chairman
Robert J. Leake, honorable secretary
36 Elliston House
100 Washington St.
Woolwich
London SE18
England

Holds meetings, dinners, film screenings and special events. Publishers a newsletter and *Voices from the Vault,* a periodical of commentaries, articles and reviews. Membership applications are approved by a board.

The Bram Stoker Society
Albert Power
227 Rochester Ave.
Dun Laoghaire
County Dublin
Ireland

Bibliography and Recommended Reading

Barber, Paul. *Vampires, Burial, and Death: Folklore and Reality.* New Haven, Conn.: Yale University Press, 1988.

Carter, Margaret L., ed. *The Vampire in Literature: A Critical Bibliography.* Ann Arbor: UMI Research Press, 1989.

Copper, Basil. *The Vampire in Legend and Fact.* New York: Citadel Press, 1973.

Dresser, Norine. *American Vampires: Fans, Victims, Practitioners.* New York: W. W. Norton & Co., 1989.

Farson, Daniel. *The Man Who Wrote Dracula: A Biography of Bram Stoker.* London: Michael Joseph, 1975.

Florescu, Radu R., and Raymond T. McNally. *Dracula: Prince of Many Faces: His Life and Times.* Boston: Little, Brown, 1989.

Fodor, Nandor. *The Haunted Mind.* New York: Helix Press, 1959.

Fortune, Dion. *Psychic Self-Defence.* York Beach, Me.: Samuel Weiser, 1957. First published 1939.

Frost, Brian J. *The Monster with a Thousand Faces: Guises of the Vampire in Myth and Literature.* Bowling Green, Ohio: Bowling Green State University Popular Press, 1989.

Garden, Nancy. *Vampires.* New York: Bantam Skylark, 1973.

Glut, Donald. *True Vampires of History.* New York: HC Publishers, 1971.

Guiley, Rosemary Ellen. *The Encyclopedia of Witches and Witchcraft.* New York: Facts on File, 1989.

Guiley, Rosemary Ellen. *Harper's Encyclopedia of Mystical and Paranormal Experience.* San Francisco: Harper San Francisco, 1991.

Herbert, W. V. *By-Paths in the Balkans.* London: Chapman and Hall Ltd., 1906.

Hill, Douglas. *The History of Ghosts, Vampires, and Werewolves.* New York: Harper and Row, 1973.

Hillyer, Vincent. *Vampires.* Los Banos, Calif.: Loose Change Publications, 1988.

Hoyt, Olga. *Lust for Blood: The Consuming Story of Vampires.* Briarcliff Manor, N.Y.: Stein and Day, 1984.

Hufford, David J. *The Terror That Comes in the Night: An Experience-Centered Study of Supernatural Assault Traditions.* Philadelphia: University of Pennsylvania Press, 1982.

Hurwood, Bernhardt J. *Vampires.* New York: Quick Fox, 1981.

Kaplan, Stephen, as told to Carole Kane. *Vampires Are.* Palm Springs, Calif.: ETC Publications, 1984.

Leatherdale, Clive. *Dracula: The Novel and the Legend.* Wellingborough, Northamptonshire: The Aquarian Press, 1985.

Leatherdale, Clive. *The Origins of Dracula.* London: William Kimber, 1987.

Lodge, Oliver. *Peasant Life in Jugoslavia.* London: Seely, Service & Co. Ltd., n.d.

MacKenzie, Andrew. *Dracula Country: Travels and Folk Beliefs in Romania.* London: Arthur Barker, 1977.

Manchester, Sean. *From Satan to Christ.* London: Holy Grail Press, 1988.

Bibliography and Recommended Reading

Manchester, Sean. *The Highgate Vampire*. Rev. ed. London: Gothic Press, 1991. First ed. published 1985.

Masters, Anthony. *The Natural History of the Vampire*. New York: G. P. Putnam's Sons, 1972.

McNally, Raymond T. *A Clutch of Vampires*. New York: Bell Publishing, 1984.

McNally, Raymond T. *Dracula Was a Woman: In Search of the Blood Countess of Transylvania*. New York: McGraw-Hill, 1983.

McNally, Raymond T., and Radu Florescu. *In Search of Dracula: A True History of Dracula in Vampire Legends*. Greenwich, Conn.: New York Graphic Society, 1972.

Perkowski, Jan L. *The Darkling: A Treatise on Slavic Vampirism*. Columbus, Ohio: Slavica Publishers, 1989.

Ravensdale, Tom, and James Morgan. *The Psychology of Witchcraft*. New York: Arco, 1974.

Rice, Anne. *Interview with the Vampire*. New York: Alfred A. Knopf, 1976.

Rice, Anne. *The Queen of the Damned*. New York: Alfred A. Knopf, 1988.

Rice, Anne. *The Vampire Lestat*. New York: Alfred A. Knopf, 1985.

Ronay, Gabriel. *The Truth about Dracula*. Briarcliff Manor, N.Y.: Stein and Day, 1972. First published 1972 as *The Dracula Myth*.

Stuart-Glennie, John S. *The Women of Turkey and Their Folklore*. London: David Nutt, 1890.

Summers, Montague. *The Vampire: His Kith and Kin*. New Hyde Park, N.Y.: University Books, 1960. First published 1928.

Summers, Montague. *The Vampire in Europe*. New York: E. P. Dutton and Co., 1929.

Twitchell, James B. *The Living Dead: A Study of the Vampire in Romantic Literature*. Durham, N.C.: Duke University Press, 1981.

Underwood, Peter. *The Vampire's Bedside Companion*. London: Leslie Frewin, 1975.

Volta, Ornella. *The Vampire*. London: Tandem, 1965.

Waller, Gregory A. *The Living and the Undead*. Urbana, Ill.: University of Illinois Press, 1986.

Bibliography and Recommended Reading

Wolf, Leonard. *The Annotated Dracula*. New York: Clarkson N. Potter, 1975.

Wolf, Leonard. *A Dream of Dracula: In Search of the Living Dead*. Boston: Little, Brown, 1972.

Wright, Dudley. *Vampires and Vampirism*. London: William Rider and Son, 1914.